Dog Massage

Also by Maryjean Ballner

Cat Massage

Dog Massage

A WHISKERS-TO-TAIL

GUIDE TO YOUR DOG'S

ULTIMATE PETTING

EXPERIENCE

Maryjean Ballner

ST. MARTIN'S GRIFFIN
New York

Photos by Erica Herbert, Rogers Staehlin, and Maryjean Ballner

Design by Patrice Sheridan

LIBRARY OF CONGRESS CATALOGING-IN-PUBLICATION DATA

Ballner, Maryjean.
    Dog massage: a whiskers-to-tail guide to your dog's ultimate petting experience /
Maryjean Ballner.—1st ed.
        p.   cm.
    ISBN 0-312-26727-4
    1. Dogs—Diseases—Alternative treatment.   2. Massage for animals.   I. Title.
    SF991.B27   2000
    636.7'0895822—dc21   00-040259

First Edition: January 2001

10   9   8   7   6   5   4   3   2   1

To my wonderful husband, Rogers

Acknowledgments

I thank God for the life I have today.

Deepest thanks to Dr. Melissa Mathews, lead veterinarian at the Peninsula Humane Society, San Mateo, California. She is an excellent, compassionate veterinarian, devoted to animals, and dedicated to animal rescue (www.ecis.com/~mmbb). I am grateful for hours of her insight and expertise in reviewing this book.

Thanks to Beth Ward, Director of Animal Care, at the Peninsula Humane Society. Her concern for animals is abundant, and second only to her knowledge about them and her willingness to share that knowledge.

Thanks to Janine Adams, Beth Adelman, Darlene Arden, Maggie Bonham, Deb Eldredge, DVM, Jill Haddan, Amy Shojai, Cheryl Smith, Amy Snow, and Chris Walkowicz for answering canine qustions.

Many thanks to Kathy Greer, J. Ronald Bean, and Alan Sommer, who helped with non-canine issues.

Thanks to my editor, Kristen Macnamara, for all her help.

Once again, thanks to Suzanne Magida for her copyediting expertise.

Thanks to Stella and Dick Krieger, from Rapid Photo, in San

Ramon, California, for evening film drop-offs and early-morning photo pickups.

Thanks always to the loving memories of my mother, Florence Ballner, and Bob Arbib, who encouraged me from the start. Thanks to my father, William Ballner, for his everyday love and concern.

A very special thanks to all the dogs with whom I've had the pleasure of sharing massage.

Special thanks to the dogs photographed for the book, and their guardians:

Shelby (yellow Lab),
Erica and Steve Herbert

Emily (greyhound), Melissa
Mathews, DVM, and Bill Bourcier

Ebony (black Lab),
Leslie and Jeff Gant

Max (Border collie),
Beth Ward and Jill Haddan

Marvin (black Lab mix),
Beth Ward and Jill Haddan

Gretchen (dachshund),
Anni and Erich Daubert

Pretzel (dachshund),
Anni and Erich Daubert

Henry Wrinkler
(shar-pei/Lab mix),
Beth Ward and Jill Haddan

Sammy (German shepherd puppy),
Sarah Ward-Haddan

Contents

Author's Note   xv

Introduction   1

What Is Dog Massage?   5

Why Dog Massage?   9

Canine Critiques: Unfriendly and Friendly Feedback   13

Doggy Disasters to Avoid: The No-No's of Dog Massage   21

When to Dog Massage?   23

Where to Dog Massage?   25

How Your Dog Works: Anatomy and Physiology Made Simple   27

Voice Massage   32

Tools of the Trade   35

Coming in for the Landing: How to Approach
    Your Dog for Massage   47

Brush Massage   50

White Glove Treatments   51

Special Considerations   52

Tips to Remember   55

Scapula, Please   57

Shoulder Strumming   59

Two-Handed Circular Shoulder Fanning   62

Shoulder Thumbing   63

Two-Finger Spine Slides   65
Two-Handed Spine Slides   67
Just Between Us Shoulder Blades   69
Post-Exercise Shoulder Circles   70

Back for More   71

The Grand *Effleurage*   73
Hand Over Hand and Down We Go:
    A Two-Handed Double Delight   76
Base Fiddling   78
Ruffling Shuffle   80
Back Horseshoes   82
Spine Tingling   84
Finger Padding Along the Vertebrae   85
Gentle Rump Thumping   87
Farewell Flourishes   89

Let's Do a Little Necking   90

Classic Pet: A Fido Favorite   92
Waving Down the Neckline   94
Cross-Neck Flicking   96
Occipital Bump Rubbing   98
Neck Horseshoes   100

Getting Into It Head First   102

Chin-Ups   104
Crowning the King/Queen   107
Check Out Those Cheeks: A Facial Favorite   108
Apex Flicking   110
Ear Nooking: aka Trace the Ear Base   112
Smoothing Over the Whisker Beds   114
Thenar Bucca Buffing   116
Emily's Forehead Favorite   118
Side of the Head Stroking   119

Side Stroking   120

Light Fur Fluffing: A Subtle, Satisfying Stroke   121
Dog Sandwich   122
Layla's Luxurious Front-to-Back Caress   123
Alternating Circular Side Waving   125
Side Palming   127

Treasure Chest   129

Breast Stroking   130
Chest Cupping   132
Buffing the Breastplate   134
Petting the Pecs   135
Underarm Tickle   136

Thigh Action   138

Thigh Thumbing   139
Post-Exercise Thigh Circles   141

Tummy Touching   143

Belly Browsing   145
Stand-Up Stomach Stroking   147

Paws and Claws   149

Paw-Claw Caress   151
Paw Sandwich   152
Tiptoeing Through the Toes   153

Tail End   154

Caudal Cuddling   156
Tail End   157

Author's Note

This book was written with the intention of helping dog guardians develop a stronger bond with their dogs.

It is imperative to understand the breed, temperament, and personality of your dog before Dog Massage. This is meant for a well-mannered dog with which you are familiar.

Dog Massage is NOT meant for an unfamiliar dog.

Please pay careful attention to the ⬧, Unfriendly Feedback signs, special notes, and cautions inserted throughout the book. The author assumes no responsibility for any injuries as a result of the information contained in this book.

This book is not meant to diagnose, treat, or cure any medical problems.

This book is not meant as an alternative to proper medical care.

Your veterinarian is the best person with whom to discuss any questions about your dog.

Dog Massage

Introduction

Welcome to the wonderful world of Dog Massage!

If the idea seems silly or a bit quirky, keep reading. I assure you that soon you will be delighted. Within these pages are *hours* of fascinating styles of touch. Included are more than fifty time-tested and dog-approved massage techniques.

Extensive research indicates that while you will probably *like* them, your dog will surely *love* them. And your dog will love *you* even more for learning them.

> We don't speak basic "bark," so the best nonverbal way we communicate with our dogs is through touch, *and the best possible touch is massage.*

Many people pet by randomly rubbing—the absentminded stroking of Dog's back while talking on the phone, or scratching Dog's head during television commercials.

I offer you something more valuable than dog petting—Dog Massage. Traditional Swedish massage techniques have been adapted for your canine's comfort. Since you already pet your dog, you already know the basics.

As a New York State Licensed Massage Therapist, I originally developed these techniques for feline friends, in *Cat Massage*. Now they've been fine-tuned for canine companions. *Dog Massage* can revolutionize the way you touch your dog.

> 🐾 **If you were offered the choice between getting petted and getting massaged, which would you choose? Massage, of course, and so would your dog.**

Your touch becomes much more interesting when it becomes massage:

Hand Over Hand and Down We Go! replaces routine strokes along the back.

Waving Down the Neckline upgrades neck rubs, and Petting the Pecs works the mighty chest muscles.

Your touch takes on new delights with Belly Browsing and Tiptoeing Through the Toes.

Check Out Those Cheeks has brought a smile to many canine faces.

Expect a few Doggy Giggles with the Underarm Tickle and Dog Sandwich.

And don't forget your dog's tail end with Tail End.

The positive response to Dog Massage is overwhelming! An expert panel of canines assisted me throughout this book. Small, medium, and large-size breeds were consulted, and each offered their expertise. Their Canine Critiques guided and fine-tuned these techniques.

Speaking of Canine Critiques, let's paws for a moment to talk about Unfriendly Feedback and Friendly Feedback signals.

Unfriendly Feedback tells you to be respectful of your dog's response to massage. There are some canines who have been bred for their defensive nature, and prefer to not be touched. Other dogs simply don't care for it.

Know your dog's behavior and temperament before you offer any massage.

Friendly Feedback says that your dog appreciates your touch and you. When tail wagging becomes excessive, call it Power Wagging. Body Flopping becomes a familiar sight. Satisfied Snoring, Nasal Torpedoes, and Doggy Grins all encourage more massage.

As you upgrade dog petting to Dog Massage, you will notice a distinct improvement in your touch. You will enjoy it, and your dog will be thrilled. This book demonstrates simple enhancements to transform your petting to magical touch.

The following pages contain an easy-to-learn, whiskers-to-tail guide to massage techniques that can revolutionize the way you touch your dog.

If you think your dog is already friendly and affectionate now—wait for the results of Dog Massage! Anyone can rub a Rover, but it takes skill to caress your canine. If your dog enjoys touching, your dog will luxuriate with massage.

Your dog deserves the best. Your dog deserves Dog Massage.

Remember that petting makes friends, but massage makes partners.

What Is Dog Massage?

Dog Massage is upgraded petting that generates amazing results.
It's quite simple, yet its effects can be quite profound.

 **Wouldn't you agree that while a touch feels good,
a caress feels better?**

Therein lies the theory of Dog Massage. First we define a technique; then we refine the technique.

Some of Dog Massage is what you already know. You'll recognize some of these techniques, because surely you already do some of them. Now they've been analyzed, named, and improved. By using a variety of hand parts, different hand positions, a diversity of motions, particular pressures, and distinct speeds, we create various moods.

Dog Massage quickly becomes more interesting than petting. By adding detail and finesse, we upgrade dog petting to Dog Massage. If you were offered an upgrade, whether you were renting a car or reserving seats on an airplane, you'd take it, wouldn't you? Let's offer that same upgrade to our dogs.

Massage Versus Petting

In the dictionary, petting is defined as rubbing. Compare that to massage. Even the term sounds more satisfying. The dictionary says that to massage is "to rub for remedial effect." It focuses more attention on your actions, to generate a desired outcome.

If you've ever enjoyed a professional massage, you know the sublime relaxation this experience brings. Skillful touch improves flexibility and circulation. Tense, overworked muscles loosen. Stiff aching joints find relief with therapeutic touch, and overall body stress is reduced.

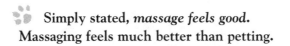 **Simply stated, *massage feels good.*
Massaging feels much better than petting.**

Massage not only feels good, it *is* good for us. Physicians and health and fitness experts around the world promote massage as enjoyable and essential to a healthy lifestyle. Shouldn't our dogs, who share all the other activities of our lives, also benefit from a regular dose of this touch therapy?

If you've never had a massage, it may be time to experience one. That way you'll know how good touch can get, and you can pass the canine equivalent along to your companion dog.

These are not deep muscle manipulations; our techniques are not intended to replace any medical treatment or relieve medical complaints. These techniques simply feel good. Dog Massage will give you new and wonderful ways to touch your companion dog. Your dog will know the difference between rubbing and massage, and your dog will want massage. Be able to offer it.

 Pet a dog, make a friend for a day. When you massage your dog, you'll make a friend for life.

History of Dog Massage

Back in 1983, I was a student at the Swedish Institute for Massage Therapy in New York City. During that time, I began consciously and unconsciously applying Swedish massage principles and techniques to my feline companion, Mr. Grey.

There was a distinct change in his personality. Once a feral cat, he slowly became friendly, responsive, and then downright affectionate.

My final paper was entitled "Massage Therapy from a Feline Point of View." I compared anatomy and physiology for humans and felines, and adapted massage strokes for their sizes and shapes.

Years later, when another cat named Champion came to live with me, I repeated the same techniques and received the same results—an incredible bonding between my companion animal and me. Even my terrified shelter cat, Bodacious, warmed up with massage.

Now these techniques have been adapted again for canines. They work equally well and bring the same wonderful responses.

I welcome you to join in the magic of Dog Massage.

Why Dog Massage?

Massage is important for improving sociability, health, and fun. I don't guarantee that massage will accomplish any specific purpose. However, from years of experience working with humans, felines, and now canines, I've seen how massage can facilitate positive change in subtle, indirect ways.

There's a special relationship that often forms between a dog and guardian when they share the bond of massage. Their connection is unique, can't be purchased, and flourishes over time. Once you experience the benefits of Dog Massage, you'll be looking for any reason to use Dog Massage. I know your dog will!

1. Dog Massage can enhance your relationship with your canine companion. Petting makes friends, but massage makes partners.

2. Routine massage sessions encourage your dog to become more involved with your family, and your family to become more involved with your dog.

3. Dog Massage is an all-new way to pay attention to your dog. Dogs crave attention, they deserve it, and massage is a great way to give it. This is especially important for those who work long hours or are away from home for extended periods of time.

4. Dog Massage is a new way to express affection for your dog. More than a fancy collar or a cute food bowl, your dog needs affection. Your dog probably already *demands* affection, so Dog Massage will show *you* the best ways to give it.

5. Massage is one of the fastest ways to build the bond between dog and guardian, which is essential for a loving relationship.

6. Puppies benefit from touch, especially during their prime socialization period, between three and ten weeks of age. The most critical period is from six to eight weeks, when puppies most easily learn to accept others as part of their family. This can help establish more tolerance in them, resulting in a better canine companion for you.

7. Changes in your dog's health may be felt before they can be seen, especially if your dog has a very furry coat. By routinely massaging, you will be clued in to any changes in your dog's coat and skin. It can alert you to any unusual growths on or below the surface of the skin and can help you detect fleas and ticks as well. Remember—an early diagnosis leads to a better prognosis.

8. Your *dog* will want a massage. Once you learn the techniques of Dog Massage, your canine companion will no longer be content with random rubbing, and neither will you.

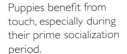

Puppies benefit from touch, especially during their prime socialization period.

9. Regular massage sessions may allow your dog to get accustomed to being handled.

10. If you need to board your dog, you can pass along the preferred Dog Massage techniques to the people who will be taking care of your dog.

11. A systematic approach of gentle massage may enable your dog to be more receptive to touch.

12. When your dog is easy to handle, veterinary visits may be less scary for the dog, you, and the vet. Everyone involved will appreciate that.

13. Along with obedience training, Dog Massage may help transform a rowdy Rover into your companionable canine.

14. Even the most arthritic hands can successfully Dog Massage their dog, and even the most senior dogs will welcome a gentle loving touch from their guardian.

15. Physiologically, massage produces an increase in blood circulation that rapidly clears away waste products and replaces them with fresh nutrients.

16. You will become more finely tuned to your dog's physical condition, with firsthand, up-to-date information. This is very important when giving medical history to the vet and discussing your dog's health.

17. When words won't work, massage may calm your panicky canine or reassure your frightened Fido. It may ease the apprehension of your high-strung dog.

18. As you become familiar with the Paws and Claws from massage, your dog *may* allow you to clip the tips of her nails—saving you time and money.

19. Grooming becomes more interesting and desirable when you combine it with Brush Massage techniques, which reward your dog with a healthier coat. Brushing can be more enjoyable for both you and Dog when combined with certain techniques, such as The Grand *Effleurage* (pages 73–75).

20. Massage relaxes muscles on your active dog.

Dog Massage is great for senior dogs and senior citizens.

Dog Massage is the fastest way to produce a Doggy Grin.

21. Massage can be both brief and effective. Four magical minutes of massage can replace twenty minutes of random rubbing.

22. Dog Massage encourages you to get creative with your touch—both you and Dog will delight in experiencing new tactile sensations.

23. Financially, it's cost-effective. This book gives you all the information you need to build and develop your own massage repertoire.

24. The necessary components of Dog Massage are always available—intent, patience, persistence, and open-mindedness.

25. Preferences change, so once you know the building blocks, you'll always be able to create new massage medleys, so your dog and you will never get bored with Dog Massage.

26. Dog Massage can be therapeutic for your dog and you.

27. Massage provides insight into your dog's personality— one way to gauge how your dog is feeling.

28. Dog Massage can encourage your dog to be more responsive to your touch.

29. Touch is powerful—it conveys love, deepens trust, and forges a relationship.

30. Dog Massage is the fastest way to produce a Doggy Grin!

31. Massage shows your love and appreciation for your best friend.

32. Bath time becomes more interesting when you use massage techniques on your soapy dog.

Canine Critiques: Unfriendly and Friendly Feedback

How to Know If You Are Giving a Good Dog Massage

Relax, you have the best teacher available, your wonderful dog. You'll see the fruits of your labor blossom as Madame or Monsieur Chien responds to your touch. Your dog will graciously provide Canine Critiques—the warning signals and guiding advice.

Look carefully, listen, and take suggestions. By learning to read your dog's reactions, a more intuitive understanding can develop between you and your dog.

 Best of all, you will be thrilled when you get a hearty "two paws up" of approval.

While dog massage is generally fun and lighthearted, this next section is extremely serious.

Signals of Unfriendly Feedback

Respecting Unfriendly Feedback can make the difference between making massage a pleasurable enjoyment shared or an ordeal endured. When your dog is hurt, displeased, scared, upset, or defensive she will give you Unfriendly Feedback signals to warn you. It is your responsibility to watch for them and act on them.

Cautions appear for certain techniques that may cause Unfriendly Feedback.

 **If Unfriendly Feedback occurs,
do not question your dog;
do not challenge your dog;
DO NOT CONTINUE.**

NOTE: If your dog bites without warning, then Dog Massage is not for you.

Signals of Unfriendly Feedback

Some are obvious, some subtle. Watch for all of them, especially the subtle. Respect every one of them.

Dog's teeth on your skin: For the safety of you and your family, there is never an appropriate time for your dog's teeth to touch your skin. *STOP massage.*

Growling: Dog is TELLING you she is uncomfortable. *STOP massage.*

Posturing: Dog holds her breath and holds still. She's figuring out what you're doing, and planning her next move in response. *STOP massage.*

Ears flattened back: More defensive body language. Again, Dog is telling you that something is wrong. *STOP massage.*

Eyebrows moving up and down: Dog is wary. *STOP massage.*

Body tensing, especially the neck: Just like humans stiffen up in defense, so do our canines. *STOP massage.*

Dog moves away: This shows an obvious lack of interest. Although it is unusual, don't take it personally—Dog may simply not be in the mood. *STOP massage.* Try again later.

Pulling away: Dog doesn't want to be a part of the action. *STOP massage.*

Whale eyes: Head turned, Dog looks at you out of the corner of her eye, exposing a majority of the white part of her eye. *STOP massage.*

Any unusual, negative, or out-of-character behavior: This means cool it for now. *STOP massage.*

Never do anything that will in any way disturb your dog.

Note: *Some Unfriendly Feedback may indicate a medical problem.* If a dog who always welcomed the Ruffling Shuffle now pulls away, perhaps there's a problem with her lower back. A hurt paw may cause another dog to reject the Paw Sandwich. Stomach disorders can make even the lightest Belly Browsing uncomfortable. Rejection of a previously enjoyed massage technique may indicate a medical problem. Do not attempt massage, and immediately consult your vet. Unfriendly Feedback warns you to *stop what you are doing.*

Watch for Unfriendly Feedback. Think of it this way—Dog is uncomfortable, so stop whatever you are doing. After each technique, there's a space to check off your dog's response. If there's Unfriendly Feedback, check off the No Thanks space and move on to another technique—there are plenty to choose from.

Be prepared for Unfriendly Feedback. In fact, look for it, because your dog will warn you before she responds unfavorably. With time and practice, this list may grow shorter as the Friendly Feedback flourishes. Your dog may enjoy forty different techniques. Or yours may enjoy three, no more. If that's the case, that's her choice. Remember who you're doing massage for—your dog.

> **Listen and follow your dog's suggestions.**
> **Adaptability and the willingness to change by**
> **following Canine Critiques are key components**
> **for Dog Massage success.**

You can always try to introduce a technique again at a later date. Go with the flow—what may be a favorite this week can drop to low stroke on the totem pole next week.

Very Important: Make it easy for Dog to share Unfriendly Feedback with you. Never get displeased or irritated because *you* like a certain technique and your dog does not. There are plenty of massage techniques, and there is plenty of Dog to massage, and you soon will find a comfortable balance between the two.

Some Unfriendly Feedback is short-term, and some is long-term. Some dogs will tolerate no Tummy Touching, yet others go belly up as soon as someone is near. Go figure. So, again, if you find one technique isn't quite your dog's delight, simply move on to another. There's plenty of your dog to massage, and plenty of massage for your dog.

Ways that my dog says No Thanks.

_____

_____

_____

_____

Signals of Friendly Feedback

Happy Dog: Your dog is happy and shows it.

Doggy Grin: We've all seen them and they're glorious.

Tail Wagging: Classic dog-approved action. From a slight breeze to a full knockdown wind, this says that your touch and you are appreciated. When wagging becomes excessive, I call this *Power Wagging*.

Body Flopping: When Dog tips herself over and flops onto one side. An experienced body flopper will do it in such a way as to not miss a single massage stroke.

Drooling: In this case, a drooler is not a person specializing in rings and watches. It's a dog who's so wrapped up in enjoying a massage that she forgets to swallow—then she drools. Silly as it may sound, this is a very expressive and unconscious approval. Remember, you can't fool drool.

Slobbering: When drooling becomes excessive, we call it good old-fashioned slobbering. Sticky for the furniture, complimentary for you.

Resting Onya: When Dog, or any part thereof, climbs up and sprawls on top of you. It may be a single paw resting on your arm or leg; it can be crowding alongside you on the couch, or edging you off the bed.

Head Butts: Dog rubs her head against your hand in anticipation of touch.

Nasal Torpedoes: Similar to head butts—this is when the nose is used exclusively. They may be direct, head-on hits, or side swipes. A very cool feedback (literally), and moist, too.

Satisfied Snoring: Some of the most welcomed nasal noise you'll ever hear.

Front Door Blocking: Dog preventing you from leaving the house—usually accompanied by a "massage toll before exiting" agreement.

Happy Dog

Resting Onya

Dog Kisses: Tender little licks and sniffing—not the out-of-control ones—these are non-traditional kisses as we know them, but definitely a canine compliment.

Deep Sigh: A long inhalation and slow steady exhalation, it's usually followed by complete inactivity. Pure bliss.

Eyes Blinking Dreamily: Soft opening and closing of eyes conveys soothing approval.

Dog Sticks Around: Not because *you* want her to, but because *she* wants to. This complimentary acknowledgment is a green light that says go ahead.

Adoring Eyes: Filled with love and affection—times when Dog looks at you with what can only be termed pure love. Isn't it great?

Response Rubbing: When Dog returns your caresses with caresses of her own. Dog will manipulate herself to accommodate your tender touching and to anticipate your next move. It's canine encouragement with direction. Around the cheek area, for example, Dog will crane her neck to guide you along and maneuver your stroke to her precise desires.

Belly Up: That triumphant time when your dog rolls over onto her back and exposes her belly, a vulnerable submissive position for her and a tribute to you.

Body Stretching: Long luxurious stretching to encourage you to continue your magic touch.

Relax and Go Limp: A dog who has just mellowed out completely.

Greeting: Your dog will be greeting you at the door upon your arrival home, ready, waiting, and willing for massage.

Vibrating Lips: Quivering jawline action, a "can't-be-faked" move that shouts approval.

Dog Demanding Massage: Reading the newspaper to find a head poking up from underneath, being licked awake from an afternoon couch nap, or a canine pleading with soulful eyes. These are the gentle nudges that tell you it's time for a massage.

Rover Repeats: Massage is finished, in your opinion, but Dog is ready for you to start all over again.

Doggy Giggles: If you listen closely, sometimes you can hear them.

Walk Later, Massage Now!: This is when Dog bypasses her leash and a walk outdoors in favor of massage time. Unusual, though it does happen.

Food Bowl Pass: An amazing compliment. When Dog actually ignores the food in her bowl, and instead follows you for affection.

Head Lifts: Slow satisfaction expressed with a head that eventually points straight up in the air in appreciation of you.

Yawning: A full, lazy yawn in gratitude for your touch.

Chin-Ups: A clear indication of technique approval. When your dog cranes her head up, chin pointing toward the sky. This is a complete canine compliment.

Other canine compliments from my dog:

_____

_____

_____

Check this list from time to time and see what changes. Check off your dog's preferences after each massage technique, in the spaces provided. Some will be My Dog Likes and others will be My Dog Really Likes. Enjoy the discovery of your favorites!

Yawning

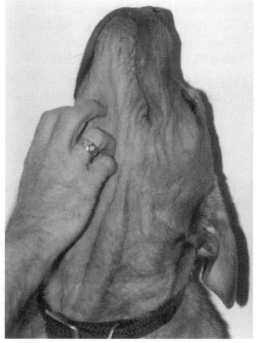

Chin-ups

Doggy Disasters to Avoid: The No-No's of Dog Massage

Just about everything associated with Dog Massage is good for your dog: any drawbacks are far outweighed by the positives. To keep it that way, included are some things to remember—and things to avoid—during Dog Massage.

- Pay attention to all Canine Critiques—especially the Unfriendly Feedback.
- *You* best know the temperament and tolerance of your canine. Don't push it to the limits, and *never* exceed it.
- Never try Dog Massage on an unfamiliar dog.
- Never force massage on a dog—it absolutely won't work, Dog will end up frustrated and angry, and so will you.
- If *you're* not in a good mood, don't Dog Massage—you'll end up frustrated and angry, and so will Dog.
- Don't wear out your welcome. When Dog decrees that massage time is over—it's over.
- Always respect your dog's boundaries. Massage according to his preferences of techniques, pressures, speeds, motions, or moods.
- No oils, creams, or lotions are necessary—just your clean hands.
- *Absolutely* never give a dog any kind of massage if you are under the influence of alcohol or drugs. Your perception is

altered more than you'll think, and the results could be disastrous or downright devastating.

- Never pull on Dog's fur, ears, or tail. Just like Mom says: "Would you like someone to do that to you?" I think not, so don't do it to your dog.
- Never pull Dog's whiskers. It is cruel, not cute. Don't do it.
- Never press deeply on Dog's stomach. You can easily damage internal organs.
- Massage with your hands, not your feet, no matter how comfortable you are with this or how long you've been doing it. This is a potential hazard just waiting to happen.
- A dog's private parts are just that—private—to be left alone and not to be touched by you.
- Never press too deeply on your dog. You'll avoid "too deeply" if you start off lightly and follow your dog's responses. Remember that we are usually much bigger and stronger than our canines.
- Watch fingernails! Long beautiful nails look lovely on a hand, but they can create big problems with scratching or scraping. Be *extra* careful, especially near sensitive, delicate areas such as ears and whiskers.
- Never substitute massage for veterinary treatment. If you are massaging a post-operative or ailing dog, do so only with the awareness and approval of your dog's veterinarian.

CAUTION

Be careful not to do too much too soon. It's a tempting human trait to run through and show off everything you've just read. Please don't do this; you'll exhaust your poor pet and yourself, too. In early massage, keep variety to a minimum.

Hopefully, you and Dog will be together for quite a while, so take your time and enjoy all that Dog Massage has to offer.

When to Dog Massage?

That's for you and your dog to discover and decide together. Dog Massage can be a few quick strokes on the way out to work, it can be four minutes of magical touch, or it can be a long, leisurely pampering session.

There may be times when your dog is not interested in Dog Massage. Respect those boundaries. Every Dog has moments of disinterest, so allow him that choice.

Some dogs, at some times, will not want a massage. If this is ever the case, STOP! Never push a massage on a dog. If Dog is not interested, don't pursue it.

Be aware: There are some dogs who may NEVER want a massage.

CAUTION

If your dog enjoys massage—consider this: Dogs like rituals. An excellent way to incorporate Dog Massage into your daily routine is to do it at a specific time every day. Each morning when coffee is brewing, for example, and before your day gets too busy, take five minutes and devote that time to focused concentration for your canine. Soon your dog will stand by, ready for your talented hands.

More often than not, your dog will determine Dog Massage times. It may be:

- Television watching—your dog's cue to be massaged, and commercials become so much more bearable with a dog curled up alongside you.

- Reading a book alone is enjoyable, but sharing it with a dog makes any book a winner.

- As soon as you walk through the door.

- The moment you wake up.

- When you are still sound asleep. You'll be nudged awake.

- When you are in the middle of an important project and can't be disturbed.

- When you are working on the computer—a few strokes for the keyboard, a few strokes for the dog.

- Whenever your dog sees you.

- As soon as you've finished the first Dog Massage, Dog wants you to start over.

- After Dog has exercised or had a good workout.

- Whenever Dog is in the mood.

- Right before bedtime—up on the blankets or under the covers.

In the beginning, you may find yourself initiating your Dog Massage sessions. But I assure you, soon your dog will want more massage. Then it's only a matter of time before your dog demands more massage. Consider it a sign of progress, and congratulate yourself.

Where to Dog Massage?

Choose a familiar place where you and your dog can be comfortable. Dog size can affect certain positions. An eight-pound poodle will sit more comfortably on your lap than an eighty-pound shepherd.

NEVER crowd your dog. Know and respect your dog's temperament and tolerance. Some dogs enjoy face-to-face contact—for others, it's threatening or a challenge of authority. Know your dog.

CAUTION

Preferred Places and Positions:

 You and Dog sitting together.

 On the couch—is your canine allowed to be a sofa dog, and do you cozy up together on the couch? If so, this horizontal position affords great opportunities. A new angle brings a new slant to massage, and encourages your dog to really extend her body with full stretches.

(Continued)

Couch potato partners become natural couch cuddling companions.

 On the floor together.

 Mr. or Miss Dog sitting on your lap—a classic massage position for smaller breeds.

 On the bed—another individual preference, since bedtime is generally a tranquil time. Some of the best Dog Massage techniques get developed in this comfortable environment. Is your dog in the habit of resting alongside you when you prepare for sleep? A long, luxurious massage will mellow you both to a contented sleep. Upon awakening, a few morning massage strokes are a great way to start your day.

Bedtime can become synonymous with massage time, and build some of your best bonding times.

On the floor together

Dog Massage is a cooperative effort with mutual rewards.

How Your Dog Works: Anatomy and Physiology Made Simple

There are only two basic components for good Dog Massage. One is you, and the other is your dog. Your part, as massager, is to supply the massaging instruments—your hands and fingers, using different motions, pressures, and speeds. Your canine companion, as massagee, provides the body.

Let's take a closer look at your dog's anatomy—the study of body structure, function, and physiology.

Your dog is a mammal of the genus *Canis familiaris*, and is a descendent of the wolf (*Canis lupus*). Your dog's anatomy is certainly quite different from ours, but all the component parts are amazingly similar. Their bones correspond to ours; their nervous system, muscles, circulation, and internal organs all function in the same way as our own.

If you know where your neck bones, your backbone, and your thigh muscles are, you can easily locate their counterparts on your dog. Because of this anatomical similarity, where massage feels good for you, it will also feel good for your dog.

Canine Anatomy: What's Where

With only a few exceptions, I'll use canine terms when referring to your dog's anatomy. I'll refer to forelegs and hindlegs, rather than arms and legs; I'll talk about paws and claws, not hands and fingernails. But as for nose, mouth, eyes, forehead, chin, throat, neck, shoulder, back, chest, and belly—your dog has them all, exactly where you'd expect them to be.

How Your Dog Works

Let's look a bit more closely at what goes on inside your dog's furry body. You'll be better with Dog Massage when you can visualize what's under the fur and how it works.

The Bones

About 320 bones form the skeletal framework around which your entire animal is constructed. Bones protects delicate structures. The skull, for example, protects the brain, and the rib cage protects the heart and lungs. The skeleton, with its system of joints, ligaments, and tendons, allows the muscles to flex the limbs that move the dog. Together they enable your dog to walk, trot, run, chase butterflies, fetch, and curl up alongside you.

The Muscles

Since massage works the muscles, you'll need to acquaint yourself with the major muscle groups. These are the voluntary muscles, the ones that respond when we consciously tell them to act. They are coordinated; they know exactly what to do. When you turn a page in this book, voluntary muscles in your arm, hand, and fingers respond to your unspoken instruction. Involuntary muscles don't rely on commands—they are automatic, like the action of the heart muscles for pumping blood, or the diaphragm for breathing.

Muscles do many things. Most obvious, of course, is that they give your dog mobility—everything from tail chasing to luxurious body stretching. Muscles also enable the body to maintain

QUICK COMPARISONS

	Humans	Dogs
Anatomy	*Homo sapiens*	*Canis familiaris*
Total bones	206	Approximately 320
Vertebral bones		
Cervical—neck	7	7 (even the tallest giraffes have 7)
Thoracic	12	13
Lumbar	5	7
Sacral	5	3
Caudal (tail)	0	2–22
Clavicle (collarbone)	1	0
Teeth	32	Puppy—28 milk teeth—no molars; 6 or 7 months—full set of 42
Method of locomotion	Biped (walking on 2 limbs)	Quadruped (walking on 4 limbs)*
Walking position	Plantigrade (on the entire sole of the foot—bears are plantigrade)	Digitigrade (on the digits— toes—of the foot, with the remainder of the foot elevated)
Olfactory mucous membrane (provides sense of smell)	5 square centimeters† (¾ square inch)	120 square centimeters (18½ square inches)
Body temperature	98.6 F / 37 C	101.3 F / 38.5 C
Breaths per minute	16–20	10–20 (up to 30 when running)
Gestation	9 months—with usually one baby	9 weeks—with 4–10 puppies
Heart rate	80 beats per minute	70–120 per minute (smaller dogs have faster heart rates)

*This enables Dog to distribute weight more evenly and achieve better balance.
†A German shepherd has about 225 million olfactory cells, a fox terrier has about 147 million, and a basset hound has about 125 million. Humans have about 500,000. Thus a suitably trained dog can pick up the scent of a person upon smelling a piece of clothing that belongs to that person.

posture; without them, your dog could not sit, stand, roll over, or do much of anything.

A single muscle acting by itself does not accomplish a complex action. Muscles work in groups. One muscle group will coordinate to flex a limb, and its corresponding muscle group will coordinate to extend it again. Therefore, in Dog Massage, you'll work on several muscle groups in a combination of massage strokes.

During normal body functioning, blood carries nutrients to the cells and removes waste products. Blood flow is increased in a massaged area, which means more nutrients and better waste removal.

The by-product of normal body metabolism is lactic acid. During exercise, more lactic acid is produced. When more lactic acid is produced than is removed, the buildup causes muscles to ache. Massage helps to move the blood, flush out some of the toxins, and relieve some of the discomfort.

Whenever possible, take a moment to explore your own muscles as you locate and massage the corresponding muscles that move your dog.

Some Major Muscles and Where They Function

Dozens of muscles, big and small, near the surface of the skin and deep in the body, are involved with all dog movements. Some you may recognize from our corresponding human muscles. There are too many muscles to list or illustrate, and certainly too many complicated Latin names to memorize. The following list represents some of the muscles you'll massage.

Face and head: For chewing, yawning, biting, swallowing, licking, and smiling: *masseter, buccinator, digastric, temporal, occipito-mandibularis.*

Neck: For neck turning, twisting, craning, and rotating: *brachiocephalicus, latissimus dorsi, trapezius.*

Ears: For drawing the ears forward: *scutularis*. For drawing the ears up and back: *auricular*.

Shoulders and forearms: For walking, running, stretching, scratching, and digging: *biceps, brachialis, deltoid, latissimus dorsi, trapezius, triceps*.

Back: For turning, raising, arching, and stretching: *latissimus dorsi, lumbodorsal fascia* (not a muscle, but serves as an anchor for many muscles), *trapezius*.

Rump and upper hindleg: For walking, running, leaping, and scratching: *biceps caudalis, femoris, gastrocnemius, gluteus medius, gluteus superficialis, quadriceps femoris, sacrococcygeus, sartorius, tensor fascia latae*.

Abdomen: Since this area is not protected by bony structure like the ribs, abdominal muscles compress the abdominal wall and hold the abdominal organs in shape: *external obliquus, rectus abdominis*.

Chest: To connect ribs to one another: *intercostal muscles*. To flex the shoulder: *pectoralis major* and *minor*.

Forepaws: For scratching, digging, and washing the face and head: *flexor digitorum* and *extensor radialis*.

Hindpaws: For leaping and scratching: *peroneus tertius* and *tibialis anticus*.

Tail: For wagging—to show love and affection: The tail action is mainly controlled by the *caudalis* and *sacrococcygeus* muscles of the lower back.

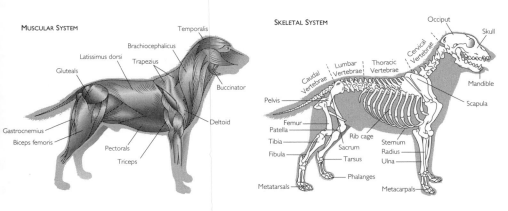

MUSCULAR SYSTEM — Temporalis, Brachiocephalicus, Latissimus dorsi, Trapezius, Gluteals, Buccinator, Gastrocnemius, Biceps femoris, Deltoid, Pectorals, Triceps

SKELETAL SYSTEM — Occiput, Skull, Cervical Vertebrae, Lumbar Vertebrae, Thoracic Vertebrae, Caudal Vertebrae, Mandible, Pelvis, Scapula, Femur, Patella, Tibia, Fibula, Rib cage, Sternum, Sacrum, Radius, Ulna, Tarsus, Phalanges, Metatarsals, Metacarpals

Voice Massage

This style of Dog Massage involves no touching at all—simply talking. You probably do Voice Massage already, at least some version of it.

When your dog is resting comfortably, do you talk quietly to him, whisper to him gently? With soothing tones, perhaps, you've repeated a familiar phrase that's special for the two of you. Some simple doggy dialogue like . . .

> You're my Rex, you're the best,
> In the north, south, east, or west.
> Oh yes, you're the best.

Add some rhythm to it and now you've got a special song.

Or you can get more elaborate and compose your own canine canticle. Here's one—add your own tune:

> Who's the best dog in the United States?
> It's you, Champer Damper, it's you.
> You're my dog and you're so good,
> You're the best dog in the neighborhood,
> You're my buddy,
> You're my friend,
> We'll be together till the very end,
> Champion and me.

This verbal caress starts a whole new response, and it's most interesting. If your hands aren't free, but you still want to communicate, try this. The results are amazingly similar to actual Dog Massage touching and the Canine Critique will be just as positive. *Voilà!* Voice Massage!

Perhaps you are already incorporating Voice Massage with your dog. Do you often find yourself talking to your dog? Can you keep up a doggy dialogue punctuated with bow-wow woofs from your canine companion? Do you stop what you're doing to talk to your handsome hound? Welcome to the world of Voice Massage!

The quality of *your* particular voice becomes so familiar, so friendly, so reassuring, and eventually so desirable.

Dog discussions range from simple phrases to complete verbal exchanges. They provide another venue for interaction and bonding. Your dog will appreciate the soothing rhythmic pattern you develop together, and it can become a lullaby of sorts.

Don't use a high-pitched voice. Ask one of your friends for a voice check. Your dog has such sensitive hearing that a high-pitched voice can cause Dog discomfort.

Practice slow, quiet, gentle talking. Your dog will appreciate it. Voice Massage can take the place of regular Dog Massage when your hands are unavailable. For telecommuters—there's no way you can ignore your dog, especially when he wants some massage.

Make Voice Massage the solution. You can work at the computer, speak quietly, continue typing, sing a song, and talk some more. Tell your canine what a good-looking pup he is, what a fine coat he's wearing, or how strong and muscular he looks. Soon he'll be curled up and complacent. Such a good life . . . another massage well done!

Create a keyword for Massage. Similar to a command, it's a word or phrase the dog will associate with the upcoming massage. Some dogs become accustomed to "Rubs!" or "Touch Time!" to signify that Dog Massage is forthcoming.

Caressing with words, soothing with sound, touching in tones—Voice Massage—whatever you wish to call it, just make sure you try it.

Tools of the Trade

Paws for a moment to become familiar with the instruments that will be doing Dog Massage—your hands. Amazing structures, each has twenty muscles and twenty-seven bones.

Certain hand parts are obvious—fingers and palms. Now explore them further—you'll be using knuckle nooks, knuckles, your thenar eminence, and all parts of your fingers.

 Instead of rubbing, think of caressing.
Now you're massaging!

Hand Parts

Some are obvious, others are new. Use all twelve! Locate them on your own hand as you read their descriptions.

Knuckles	*Thenar eminence*	*Open palm*	*Two fingers*
Knuckle nooks	*Finger pads*	*Finger sides*	*Four fingers*
Thumb	*Thumb pad*	*Closed palm*	*Fingertips*

Knuckles: Bend your fingers and notice how three rows of knuckles form. One set of knuckles is close to your fingernails. The other set of knuckles is above the first. These are the two sets of Dog Massage knuckles to use. The third row of knuckles, close to the base of your fingers, aren't used.

Knuckle nooks: Knuckles nooks form when you bend your fingers together, making a fist. That forms two knuckle nooks. The first knuckle nook is the short flat surface formed between your two finger knuckles. The other knuckle nook is the broader surface extending back up to your fist knuckles.

Thumb: Either thumb, its tips and sides.

Thenar eminence: This is the technical name for a familiar hand part. Look at your hand, palm up. The fleshy mound below the thumb is your thenar eminence. Thenar means relating to the palm, and eminence means height.

Finger pads: These are the soft, cushiony parts of the fingers—they house your fingerprints.

Thumb pad: The soft cushiony part of your thumb, right where your thumbprint is seen.

Open palm: Full hand, from fingertips to wrist, with fingers spread wide.

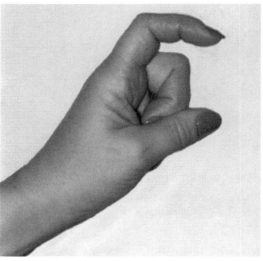

Hand Parts: knuckle nooks, knuckles

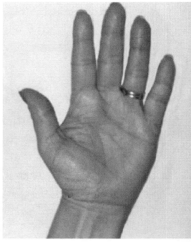

Hand Parts: open palm, thenar eminence thumb pad, finger pads

Finger sides: A different touch is made by using only the sides of each finger, so use them too.

Closed palm: Same as open palm, but with fingers closed together.

Two fingers: Use half of four fingers—two, usually the index and middle.

Four fingers: Simply use four fingers together—index, middle, ring, and pinkie—open or closed.

Fingertips: The area located above the finger pads: some end at the top of your fingers, or if you have long nails, at the tip of your fingernails.

Hand Positions

You'll be holding and curving your hands in six new positions:

Cupping   *Horizontal*   *Palm up*
Horseshoe   *Vertical*   *Palm down*

Cupping: All five fingers are together, curved, in a cupped position. Palm up creates a resting place for your dog's head or chin. Palm down, your cupped hand rests on the neck or spine.

Horseshoe: Curve four fingers together. Keep your thumb separate and still curved. A horizontal horseshoe creates the letter C and a vertical horseshoe creates an upside-down letter U.

Vertical: The palm faces lengthwise along the dog—in the illustration on page 38, your fingertips are pointing toward the dog's head with your palm parallel to the spine.

Horizontal: The palm is positioned sideways across the dog—fingertips pointing up toward the spine.

Palm up: The palm portion faces up—you see your fingerprints.

Palm down: The palm portion faces down—you see your fingernails.

The Hand Positions are suggested *starting positions*. Once you're comfortable with a technique, alternate your positions in creative diversity.

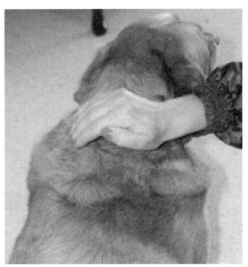

Hand Position: Cupping

Hand Position: Horseshoe

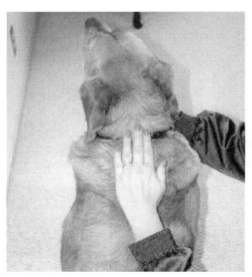

Vertical Hand Position

Horizontal Hand Position

Motions

Now you'll focus on action—which way and in which direction a technique will work best.

These six motions distinguish petting from massage. Use them as building blocks for your repertoire:

Gliding	*Circling*	*Kneading*
Waving	*Flicking*	*Rubbing*

As corny as it may sound, take a moment to practice these motions—perhaps on a pillow or a stuffed animal. You don't want to be ruffling anyone's fur when you mean to give a graceful gliding motion. Now call your dog over. It's time for massage!

Gliding: Your dog probably already enjoys these long, loving caresses. Gliding is the classic massage stroke—a long, flowing continuous motion. The direction is always toward the tail, down along the length of the body. Follow the contours of your dog, and feel for the muscles and bones. Take your hand off Dog at the end of the stroke, then bring it back up, and glide down again. If you choose to keep your hand *on* your dog during the return stroke, make sure you lighten the pressure for a distinct difference.

This is the simplest of all massage strokes, and the one most frequently used. The name of the corresponding human massage stroke for gliding is the French word *effleurage* (eff-floor-**ahj**). It works just as well on dogs as on people. In massage school, we had a saying: "When in doubt, *effleurage*." Same with gliding—you can never go wrong with gentle gliding. It always fits in.

Gliding works with any hand part. Begin your first practice strokes on a flat, broad area of Dog like the shoulders. Use slow speeds and mild pressures. Glide with your palm (open or closed), then a few times with fingertips and finger pads. It feels familiar, doesn't it? And now that you've begun to pay more attention to the style of your touch, you'll start to enjoy more benefits. Advance to using your knuckles and knuckle nooks. Try thumb gliding—you may not cover as much area, but you'll offer your dog a new sensation, and that's the essence of Dog Massage. So try it now! An entire massage session can be built with gliding. It's a great all-around, all-purpose, stroke.

Waving: Compare the side-to-side rocking motion of your hand, with fingers kept flat, to the action of a windshield wiper, or waving good-bye. This is waving, our second massage stroke. Fingers can be kept together or spread wide, using the same pressure back and forth, and either vertical or horizontal. With vertical waving, your hand sweeps along the *length* of Dog, with your fingers in the same direction as the spine. With horizontal waving, your palms or fingers sweep *alongside* Dog's body, with fingers pointing up toward the spine, then toward the tail. Waving works well on flat, broad areas, like the back and sides.

Advanced Waving technique: *Strumming.* When you're comfortable and practiced with waving, and you want a variation, try strumming. Like strumming a banjo, this is the same motion as waving, but with the tips of the fingers bent. Slow finger pad and fingertip strumming work well on smaller areas, such as the head and neck. Even knuckle nooks can be used for this stroke. You dog will delightedly help you determine the details.

Circling: Just like the name suggests, this is creating circles. Make tiny circles, barely the size of a dime, with your fingertips. Or make slightly larger circles, half-dollar shaped, with your finger pads. Watch tender areas like the ears and whiskers. Two fingers or four fingers flat together make even larger circles on a wider area, such as the shoulders, back, or sides—your choice.

Circling variation: Here's a neat idea—another simple, subtle technique that makes the difference between dog petting and Dog Massage. In addition to clockwise circles, do another series of circles *counterclockwise*. Reversing the usual direction adds an interesting twist—er, circle—to the technique. As in the case of the other motions, all your different hand parts can be used, depending on your experience and expertise.

Flicking: This involves the fingers rather than the entire hand. Imagine flicking many crumbs off a table, one by one. Or imagine flicking to be the motion created by pressing down on a pump dispenser. Flick with one, two, or three fingers, depending on the area. The thumb usually flicks alone. Light flicking barely makes contact with fur. Mild flicking allows you to feel the body underneath, and deep flicking actually moves muscle.

Kneading: Now, wait a moment here, I'm not talking about the kind of manipulating a baker performs when preparing loaves of bread (unless yours is a *big* dog). My kneading is a gentle caress, a squeezing, almost "milking" motion. Hands

Knead your dog, and your dog will need you.

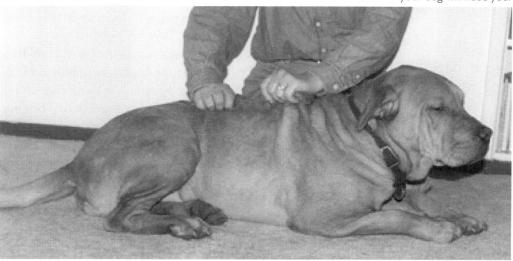

are in the vertical horseshoe position—an upside-down let-ter U. Gently grasp a loose furry area—like the scruff of the neck—in your hands. With the left hand, slowly squeeze fingers and thumb together and gently pull up. Be sure you don't pinch the skin at the end of your pull. As the left hand pulls up, your right hand opens slightly and dips down into the fur. When your left hand is pulled up, release and dip down. Now your right hand will be pulling up. Alter-nate this dip-squeeze pull-release. Get a rhythm. When the left hand is in the dip-squeeze phase, the right will be in the pull-release phase. Try it. I guarantee it's harder to explain it than it is to do. You'll soon recognize the routine and this is a great time to ask your dog for guidance.

Rubbing: This is gentle touching. Use what you've learned so far, using different hand parts and positions to make your rubbing more interesting. Create a special two-thumbed rubbing called thumbing. Use slow rubs back and forth with alternate thumbs, just like twiddling your thumbs. Thumbing works so well it even has two tech-niques designed for it—Shoulder Thumbing and Thigh Thumbing.

Another interesting idea: Once you're familiar with a hand part, alternate which *hand* you use. If you're right-handed, try us-ing your left hand. And lefties, use your right. It's just another subtle way to make Dog Massage more interesting for both of you. Now that hand parts, hand positions, and motions have been addressed, it's time to add a few more ingredients into our banquet of Dog Massage delights—speeds, pressures, and moods.

Speeds

With so much racing around that we do each day, Dog Massage becomes a welcome respite from the activity in our lives. The different speeds of Dog Massage reflect this.

Some speeds create soothing, peaceful times, some perk up your dog and you, and others set the pace for a vigorous massage—a workout for both of you. Here are our four speeds for Dog Massage:

Slow-mo   *No-mo*   *Leisurely*   *Fast 'n' Frisky*

Slow-mo (*slow motion*): "Easy does it" is a good way to live life and a great way to Dog Massage. It goes against our natural pace of rush, rush, rush. Slow-mo encourages you to pay more attention to the details of what you're doing. It's great for areas like the head and neck.

 Very Important—What may seem excruciatingly slow to you can feel so appropriate to your dog.

Do a technique you're already familiar with, like stroking Dog along the length of his back. Time yourself—how many seconds did it take? Four, perhaps? To get an idea of Slow-mo, *double* that time and repeat that stroke, taking eight seconds. It may be uncomfortable for you to work so slowly, but for many techniques, your dog will probably prefer that speed. In general, you can never go too slowly.

 Learn the art of slow stroking—it's called "go for the slow."

No-mo (*no motion*): This is even slower than slow-mo. In fact, it's just what the name implies—no motion at all. What a tricky concept for humans to understand. Too often, we are compelled to do something. We are conditioned to think that action is always imperative. But sometimes the best touch will be simply letting your fingers, palm, hand, or arm comfortably rest upon your dog. That's it—no motion, no movement necessary. Surely your dog has come over to you, parked himself, and extended his paw over your arm or leg? Just to feel you feels good to him. (Of course, with larger dogs, the leg lock may be a bit confining.) Dogs understand the concept of no-mo. In fact, many build a good part of their daily schedule around it. During a no-mo moment, a bonding occurs from just being together. Feel the rhythmic motion of your dog's breathing, follow the rise and fall of his respiration. If your dog is snuggled up against you, he'll feel the same with you. Simply allow Dog the still warmth of you resting with him.

Variation: Actually *encourage* no-mo moments. In a cupping position (page 37), offer your hand under Dog's chin as a resting place for his head. Allow him to position his front paws on top of your arm. Be still and be peaceful with your dog. Allow the idea of no-mo to become appealing. It will.

Leisurely: Just like a leisurely stroll, this is a comfortable pace. A leisurely pace enjoys gently weaving in and around your dog's contours. Phrases like "comfortable caressing" and "tender touching" come to mind. Enjoy this as a comfortable medium among the speeds.

Fast 'n' frisky: When lively massage is called for, this is the speed you want. Certain techniques specify your touch to be fast 'n' frisky, like the ruffling motion of Base Fiddling (page 78). Work this speed on broader areas, like the shoulders and back.

Pressures

Alternate your pressures. They are:

Featherlight   *Light*   *Mild*   *Deep*

The amount of pressure used is particular for each dog. Some smaller dogs enjoy deep pressures, and some larger dogs prefer light and featherlight. Work with your dog to determine his individual preferences. And remember, these change. Watch for Unfriendly and Friendly Feedback for guidance.

Featherlight: "Oh, lighten up." This is subtle stroking, barely making contact with your dog. Just feel for fur. Featherlight pressure generates interesting responses. It's ethereal, like the touch of a fairy.

Light: This is comfortable caressing and tender touching. With light pressure you'll feel fur and some of the anatomical landmarks below, like the occiput (bump at the back of Dog's head) or broad areas like the belly. Light pressure is calm, soothing, and gentle.

Mild: This is working a bit deeper. Once you're comfortable with your dog's preferences, you'll use this pressure more often. It's the pressure for locating and feeling the bony landmarks under the fur. With practice, mild pressure allows you to feel the ridges of the scapula, explore the bumpy protuberances along the spine, and examine the smooth contours of your dog's head.

Deep: Great for broad flat areas. The shoulders love deep work and so does the back. Be more careful—deeper work demands focused attention and constant dog approval. Slow deep work is more exploratory and probing; fast deep work is more energetic. As always, follow your dog's feedback.

Moods

Keep in mind the type of mood you wish to create. With purposeful petting, you can shift moods, from mellow calm right up to enthusiastic. Here are three Dog Massage choices:

Gentle and relaxed   *Playful*   *Frolicky fun*

Gentle and relaxed: Soothing, what you would expect from long, luxurious slow-mo stroking. Great for early morning wake-ups or sleepy bedtime cuddling. This mood encourages you to become as gentle and relaxed as your dog.

Playful: A leisurely paced, lighthearted mood. Both massager and massagee are enjoying themselves, having fun, and it shows.

Frolicky fun: Animated, amusing, and enthusiastic—it's hard to tell who's enjoying the massage more!

The best Dog Massage is not perfectly coordinated, planned, or choreographed. Follow sequences as they come up, or go with the flow and create your own marvelous massage medleys. Your dog will keep you clued in to what's good, better, and best.

 You and your dog are masters of your massage domain. Go for it!

Coming in for the Landing: How to Approach Your Dog for Dog Massage

CAUTION

Note: This is intended for you and your family dog, a canine companion with whom you are familiar, and whose breed and temperament is known to you. Do *not* try this with an unfamiliar, unfriendly, or unpredictable dog.

CAUTION

If your dog has an unpredictable temperament or an aggressive nature, Dog Massage is not for you.

Before you begin a massage or touching of any kind, you need to alert your dog to your intentions. Dogs appreciate a gradual approach, and their instincts *demand* one. It also shows your consideration, respecting your dog's boundaries.

Don't catch your dog off-guard, because surprising a dog is

never appropriate. Even with your faithful family dog, the pooch you've had forever, be sure to establish some form of verbal contact, with a massage keyword or Voice Massage, before your first touch. Always approach your canine companion with caution and respect. Keep in mind that there is *never any rush to any part of Dog Massage*. These steps may feel so slow. But what seems excruciatingly slow to us can feel very appropriate to our dogs.

Every dog deserves a gentle, respectful approach, and here's how dogs taught me the *Seven Steps to a Safe Approach:*

1. Initiate contact with some sort of massage keyword or "Voice Massage"—even a phrase as simple as "Hello, you good-looking dog" alerts Dog to your presence and intention to touch.
2. Always drop your hand, to Dog's eye level or lower.
3. Slowly bring your hand in closer for Dog to recognize and accept you before continuing.
4. Wait a moment—perhaps Dog will initiate first touch by rubbing her face or cheek against your hand.
5. Check for Unfriendly Feedback, which denotes caution.
6. Check for Friendly Feedback, which indicates desire and interest—tail wagging, ears perking up, or a look of anticipation.
7. Initiate your first touch on a safe, nonthreatening part of the body, like the shoulder. Begin with a few seconds of slow Shoulder Strumming.

Allow for that necessary moment of awareness and agreement. This gives Dog a chance to get involved, too. And if she decides she's not interested, do not Dog Massage. This initial contact between your dog and your hand is important. Make your approach *gentle, slow,* and *unthreatening.*

If you are not feeling comfortable with a technique, try checking each component. It may give you the answer:

Hand parts: Perhaps you are using full palm, when two or four fingers would feel better (especially on a smaller dog).

Hand positions: A horizontal or vertical position may make a distinct difference on a sensitive dog. With the horseshoe position (letter C), make sure your thumb doesn't catch on or poke any part of Dog.

Motions: Perhaps you are flicking on a sensitive area like the cheeks, where circling would feel more appropriate.

Pressures: Pressures that are too deep can hurt. Likewise, some pressures can be too light for a dog and feel uncomfortably ticklish.

Speeds: You can probably never go too slow-mo or too no-mo. But you certainly can overdo and overuse leisurely or fast 'n' frisky.

Moods: If you want frolicky fun and Dog wants gentle and re-laxed, there's a conflict of interest. Follow Dog's lead.

Be careful of tender areas—maybe you're moving too close to the eyes, or your hand is hitting against an ear. Jumping too quickly from one body part to another can be disconcerting to a canine. Trying too much too soon is another common mistake.

 Remember the basics: Go slow and repeat.
Then go slower and repeat again.

Brush Massage

Daily brushing is recommended for your dog. Grooming removes extra fur and keeps the coat naturally well oiled. Dog Massage techniques may make your brushing routines tolerable for some dogs, and thoroughly enjoyable for others.

Use the same guidelines—begin slowly and patiently, with light pressure. Follow Dog's contours and get creative. Your dog may delight in the new sensations of the brush. There's more fun to this necessary health regimen than you might expect when you combine it with Dog Massage.

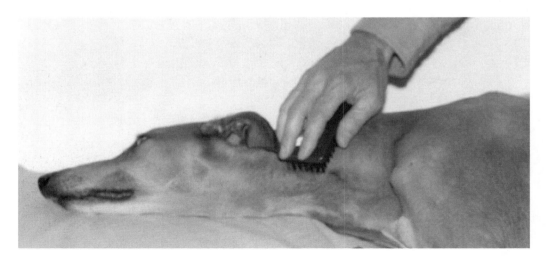

White Glove Treatments

Gloves create different textures for your skin. Wear them during a massage for a different feel, especially around Dog's face.

To feel the difference yourself, rub your fingertips along the top of your palm. Then wear a glove and repeat.

Basic winter wool gloves work well and so do mittens. It's a great way to use those stray gloves you end up with after every winter season. Thin driving gloves and very thin cotton gloves from photography supply stores also work just fine.

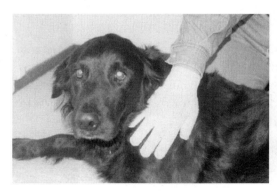
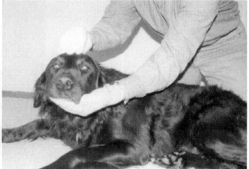

Special Considerations

The Wisdom of Age:
Senior Stroking

Senior citizens are the wisest of all of us. Whether four-legged or two-legged, they deserve every major and minor consideration possible. Even the most arthritic hands can Dog Massage, and even the most aging canine will welcome that caress. Most speeds, understandably, will be slower and the mood mostly gentle and relaxed. Nobody, whether canine or human, is too old for touch. Studies in nursing homes prove how necessary and valuable touch is for our elderly people. If studies were done among the older dog population, no doubt the same facts would hold true.

Older dogs need to be given consideration and understanding for their age. They may not react as quickly as a puppy or be as cute as a puppy, but just like our elderly people, they have a special beauty and joy reserved for their special age. Look for it, it's there. Treat them with kindness and patience. They deserve it.

Ailing and Recuperating:
Dogs and People

An injured animal instinctively licks and rubs a hurt area, just as a mother lovingly strokes her sick child. When we are sick, there's nothing like a soothing touch to help us feel better. That's why TLC—tender loving caresses—goes so far to speed up recovery. Laughter may be the best medicine, but Dog Massage runs a close second.

Never massage an inflamed area or one where your dog reacts in pain. If there is any question about your dog's health, take your dog to a veterinarian. With a terminally ill dog, under veterinary guidelines, Dog Massage can offer soothing relief.

Take the extra knowledge about your canine's condition that you've learned from your massage to the veterinarian for proper diagnosis and treatment. If your dog is injured, proper veterinary care is needed. There may be medical reasons to wait before continuing Dog Massage. Always consult with your veterinarian to make sure you are helping, never hurting, your dog.

Postsurgical

For population control and health reasons, dogs should be spayed or neutered. After this procedure, as with any surgery, ask your vet how soon you can resume Dog Massage. Although you won't be directly massaging the affected site, massaging other areas can help the recovery process.

Your dog may become unpredictable during illness, or act out of character and want no contact whatsoever. Always gauge Unfriendly Feedback as you touch your dog. If there's ever any doubt how your dog is reacting, stop massage.

People who are ailing may find great comfort in their dog's attention or even mere presence. Some dogs instinctively sense if you are sick and do their best to curl up with you and help you back to health. If you have a simple case of the blues or a cold, or you are simply flat on your back, the companionship of your dog is invaluable.

Likewise, an ailing dog may take great comfort with your loving touch. Now is the best time for slow-mo and no-mo speeds. Sometimes, just resting together is all that's needed. Dogs and humans both welcome the healing power of massage; massage is truly therapeutic touch.

Tips to Remember

 If you like dogs, you'll adore Dog Massage.

 Unless specifically doing a leisurely pace, or a fast 'n' frisky technique, work slowly.

 Honor your dog's responses and respect boundaries.

 Repeat, repeat, repeat—dogs love rituals, especially in their massages.

 This book is meant to be suggestive only. If you are thorough from the start, you'll be amazed at the canine compliments you'll receive.

 Variety—of hand parts, hand positions, motions, pressures, speeds, and moods—is the spice of life and Dog Massage.

 Patience and persistence make perfect Dog Massage technique. Practice with patience, and perfect with persistence.

 Keep your intent clear—your dog's comfort and well-being.

(Continued)

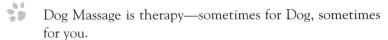 Dog Massage is therapy—sometimes for Dog, sometimes for you.

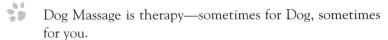 Occasionally return to basics—update and refresh yourself and your techniques.

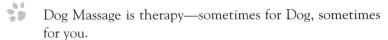 It is necessary to always start gentle and relaxed, but it's not always necessary to go faster.

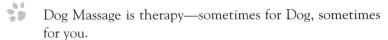 Remember, a good massage starts slow and can finish faster. A great massage starts slow and finishes slow.

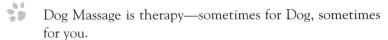 It's not what's right or wrong, it's what works.

Enjoy, enjoy, enjoy!

Scapula, Please

The shoulder is a great introductory area for massage and my favorite place to start. The shoulder joint is one of the busiest parts of your dog. Imagine it as a major intersection of muscles. The shoulder's major bone is the scapula. Located on the side of the body, it is a large, long bone, with prominent ridges, crests, curves, and grooves. It anchors more than thirty muscles, tendons, and ligaments that function in the shoulder area. This is a busy and sophisticated muscular location, and is always in use when your dog is moving.

The shoulder joint bears the heaviest weight of your dog—its front end, acting as a shock absorber for the weight. The intricate muscular design allows your dog his trademark strength and versatility. Much of a dog's movement is forward-backward motion, what we see when he walks or runs. The shoulder joint's flexibility enables a dog to twist and turn quickly, and to change direction suddenly in mid-run.

Shoulder work will be an important part of your dog's massage routine. Think for a moment how good you feel when someone rubs your aching shoulders. Although most dogs' shoulders don't hurt from being hunched over a desk for hours every day, they do tire in their daily activities. Hole digging, climbing, and running all have certain fatigue factors.

Massage in this area will start off gentle and relaxed, as always. However, this area allows for deeper exploration, as you are invited to gently probe in and around this complex musculature.

Pay attention to the grooves between the spine and the scapula, and feel the muscles with an assortment of hand parts, pressures, and speeds. Use all twelve hand parts and all six motions. And since there are two shoulders, work one shoulder, then the other. With some techniques, you can work both shoulders at the same time.

Shoulder Techniques

1. Shoulder Strumming
2. Two-Handed Circular Shoulder Fanning
3. Shoulder Thumbing
4. Two-Finger Spine Slides
5. Two-Handed Spine Slides
6. Just Between Us Shoulder Blades
7. Post-Exercise Shoulder Circles

Shoulder Strumming

AREA: Side of shoulder.

HAND PARTS: Finger pads, knuckle nooks, fingertips, two fingers, four fingers, open palms, closed palms, thenar eminence.

HAND POSITIONS: Horizontal, vertical.

MOTIONS: Gliding, rubbing, waving, circling.

SPEEDS: Slow-mo, no-mo, leisurely, fast 'n' frisky.

PRESSURES: Light, featherlight, mild, deep.

MOODS: Playful, frolicky fun, gentle and relaxed.

This stroke is a great technique, whether Dog is standing, sitting, or resting on his side. As long as you can get to the shoulder, you've got it!

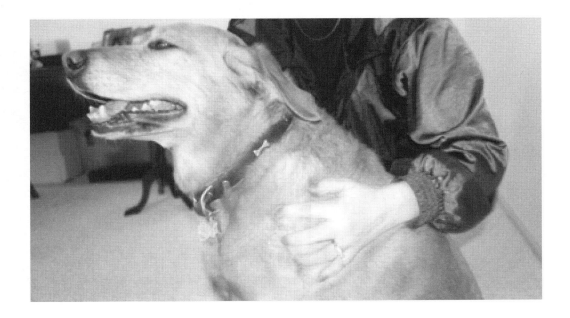

TECHNIQUE:

Feel to locate your dog's shoulders, and caress the area with a slow, downward gliding motion. Do this at least five times. Keep pressure on the descending glide, and return back with a lighter pressure.

Do a few glides with finger pads. Next use knuckle nooks. Then use fingertips, then two fingers and four fingers. Even use open palms and closed palms—let your thenar eminence rub the shoulder area as well. Notice the size and shape of the scapula, and feel its different crests and ridges.

Are you aware of different sensations
you feel from using different hand parts? Which ones
do _you_ prefer? Tiny contact from fingertips or total
contact with full palms? Watch Dog's response—
is there a preference?

Next, change gliding to its more advanced form: strumming. Instead of taking your hand off Dog at the end of the stroke, keep your hand on as you stroke up and down. Bend your fingers, and just like strumming a banjo, work the shoulder area. Start slow-mo and then build up speed to fast 'n' frisky.

Take a few minutes with each change to
really feel the differences. Remember that there is no
rush with Dog Massage. At the beginning of Dog Massage,
your canine would probably prefer one technique
repeated over and over in a variety of ways,
and Shoulder Strumming is a great
introductory technique.

When you're both ready for a change of pace, switch from gliding to waving. Like the action of a windshield wiper, wave your fingers or palm with a side-to-side rocking motion. Wave slowly and feel the bony protuberances of the area. Wave more quickly to stimulate blood flow and to work those muscles! As with gliding, wave with different finger parts—start small with finger pads or fingertips to cover a small area of the scapula. Then do that same motion with full palm. Depending on your dog's size, your palm may even cover the scapula.

Now try circling. Circle the shoulder with delightful caresses. Circle clockwise *and* counterclockwise. You can take a full ten minutes with just this technique as you examine and explore all the various components—hand parts, hand positions, motions, pressures, and speeds.

Emphasize different pressures, too. Start with light pressure, where you feel the bones and landmarks under the skin. Change to featherlight pressure, just feeling the top surface of your dog's fur. Then increase to mild pressure. Finally, deep pressure can feel great here, too.

 As always, follow your canine's critiques for best results.

There is no speed limit in the shoulder area. Start off with slow-mo, going nice and easy to become familiar with the territory. You can even go no-mo, just holding Dog's foreleg, with no action necessary. When you and Dog are more comfortable, turn up the speed to a leisurely pace, weaving in and around your dog's contours. Then accelerate up to fast 'n' frisky. The shoulder allows for vigorous massage strokes, with Shoulder Strumming as a good example.

During the day and after a workout, you can use this stroke to create a playful mood, and certainly one of frolicky fun. Slow everything down, and you'll produce a gentle and relaxed setting.

No Thanks _____   My Dog Likes _____   My Dog Really Likes _____

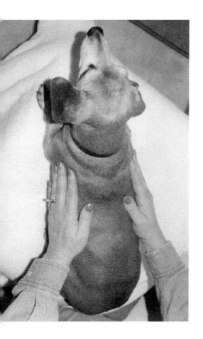

Two-Handed Circular Shoulder Fanning

AREA: Shoulder area.
HAND PARTS: Knuckle nooks, thenar eminence, finger pads, fingertips, four fingers, palms open or closed.
HAND POSITIONS: Horizontal, vertical.
MOTIONS: Circling, gliding.
SPEEDS: Slow-mo, leisurely, fast 'n' frisky.
PRESSURES: Light, mild, deep.
MOODS: Gentle and relaxed, playful, frolicky fun.

TECHNIQUE:

Pick one hand part from the list. Start slow-mo to feel contours of the shoulder area. Massage a clockwise circle along one shoulder. Make small dime-sized ones, barely moving your hand at all. Then go larger until the circle covers the perimeter of the scapula. Repeat circles about six times. In this technique, when you are using the smallest circles, your motion will cover so little area that it may feel almost like a vibration. *Vive la différence!*

VARIATION:

Work with counterclockwise circles and notice how counterclockwise feels. Vary your speeds. Does your dog enjoy a leisurely speed or life in the faster lane with fast 'n' frisky?

VARIATION:

Coordinate this technique with two hands. For a new twist, start with both hands at the top part of the shoulder. Glide your hands around simultaneously, then alternate—have one hand at the top while the other is at the bottom. Then alternate again—go counterclockwise.

No Thanks _____   My Dog Likes _____   My Dog Really Likes _____

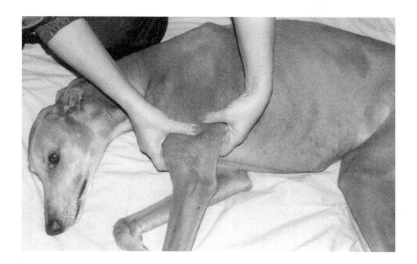

Shoulder Thumbing

AREA: Outside part of the shoulder, from the upper foreleg to the spine.
HAND PARTS: Thumbs.
HAND POSITION: Horseshoe.
MOTION: Rubbing.
SPEEDS: Slow-mo, leisurely.
PRESSURES: Light, featherlight, mild, deep.
MOOD: Gentle and relaxed.

TECHNIQUE:

With your two hands in a horseshoe position, hold Dog's foreleg. Your pinkie fingers will be closer to the body of the dog, and your thumbs will be closer to the paw. The rubbing motion will be toward the paw. Hold Dog's leg loosely but securely, with the leg resting on your palm and fingers. As if you're twiddling your fingers, slowly start rubbing with your thumbs. Rub thumbs in unison, or alternate. Start slowly and build to a leisurely speed. Start with light pressure and alternate with featherlight, mild, and deep.

🐾 **Particularly after a strenuous workout,
slow, deep work here will help flush out accumulated
toxins. Note: When done to flush out toxins, reverse
positions, so those strokes are *toward* the main body.**

Work the entire leg, starting high up near the shoulder, and continue down to the paws. The closer toward the toes, the lighter you work, because you don't want to hinder the blood's return to the heart.

You can also do this on the hindleg (Thigh Thumbing, page 139), being more careful because of heightened sensitivity in the hindquarters.

No Thanks _____   My Dog Likes _____   My Dog Really Likes _____

Two-Finger Spine Slides

AREA: Along both sides of the spine, from the neck down to the shoulder blades.

HAND PARTS: Finger pads, thumb pads, thumbs.

HAND POSITION: Vertical.

MOTION: Gliding.

SPEED: Slow-mo.

PRESSURES: Light, mild, deep on approval.

MOODS: Gentle and relaxed, playful.

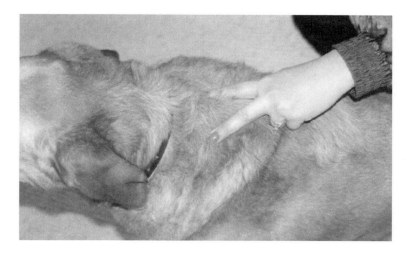

TECHNIQUE:

Use your index and middle finger pads of one hand. Position them on either side of the spine, resting them in the groove between the vertebrae (spine) and the scapula. Begin near the base of the head and slide your finger pads down the cervical spine to the shoulder blades. Let your fingers sink into this area. Slowly glide up and down, *very slowly*. Start with quarter-inch glides and increase size slowly. With larger dogs, you have more territory to cover. Probe deeper—if Dog allows—and explore this specific area carefully. Alternate, using your thumb and thumb pads. When you use your thumb, rest the part of your palm below your pinkie along Dog, to guide your hand along. If your fingernails are long, flatten your fingers so that your pads sink in, not the tips.

CAUTION

If your dog objects or moves away when you run your fingers or hand along the spinal area, it could indicate an underlying problem. Consult your veterinarian.

No Thanks _____   My Dog Likes _____   My Dog Really Likes _____

Two-Handed Spine Slides

AREA: Along both sides of the spine, from the neck down to
   the shoulder blades.
HAND PARTS: Closed palms.
HAND POSITION: Vertical.
MOTION: Gliding.
SPEED: Slow-mo.
PRESSURES: Light, mild, deep on approval.
MOODS: Gentle and relaxed, playful.

TECHNIQUE:

Position closed palms on the back, resting them along both
sides of the spine.

Begin near the base of the head and glide your palms down
the cervical spine to the shoulder blades, resting into this area.

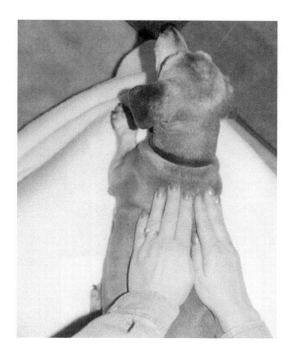

Slowly glide up and down, using light to mild pressure. Sink in a bit deeper—if Dog allows.

VARIATION:

Alternate direction of the palms—have one gently pressing up to the head while the other is pulling down toward the body. Create a smooth, slow, fluid gliding motion with your two palms. Start out gentle and relaxed and build up to playful.

CAUTION

If your dog objects or moves away when you run your fingers or hand along the spinal area, it could indicate an underlying problem. Consult your veterinarian.

No Thanks _____   My Dog Likes _____   My Dog Really Likes _____

Just Between Us Shoulder Blades

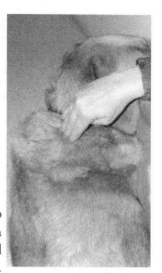

AREA: Ridge between the shoulder blades and the spine.
HAND PARTS: Fingertips, finger pads.
HAND POSITION: Palm down.
MOTIONS: Rubbing, circling.
SPEEDS: Slow-mo, leisurely.
PRESSURES: Light, mild, deep.
MOOD: Gentle and relaxed.

TECHNIQUE:

Slide one or more fingers from the back of the head/neck down to the ridge between the shoulder blades. Let your fingertips sink in slowly, and feel the complex arrangement of muscles, tendons, and ligaments as you rub Dog. Work your finger pads gently among them.

Press into a specific spot and hold the pressure for a few moments. Gauge your pressure—light, mild, or deep—by your dog's response. Weave your fingers around, making tiny circles.

Repeat using fingertips. (Always be cautious with fingernails.) Massage back and forth and side to side in this active area.

Do not start shoulder work with this technique. Do some massage to warm up Dog and shoulder before you do this technique.

CAUTION

No Thanks _____   My Dog Likes _____   My Dog Really Likes _____

Post-Exercise Shoulder Circles

AREA: Shoulder blade area.
HAND PARTS: Open palm, finger pads, four fingers.
HAND POSITIONS: Vertical, horseshoe.
MOTIONS: Rubbing, circling, gliding.
SPEEDS: Slow-mo, leisurely with Dog approval.
PRESSURES: Light, mild, deep with Dog approval.
MOODS: Gentle and relaxed, playful.

This is an advanced technique for Doggy after-workout action. Our veterinarian recommends it to help prevent shoulder stiffness in the high-action dog. This technique soothes the powerful shoulder muscles that lie on the scapula and bring the leg forward and back.

TECHNIQUE:

Vertically position your open palm to rest on the scapula in a horseshoe position. Press in with light pressure and push up to the rounded top edge of the scapula. Gently rub your finger pads in the area, then make tiny circles. Release pressure. Then move down a bit toward the bottom of the scapula. Sink in with light pressure again. Gently rub your finger pads in the area, making tiny circles. Increase pressure to mild or deep with Dog's approval. Keep speed slow-mo, leisurely with Dog's approval. Create a gentle and relaxed mood and build to playful with Dog's approval.

 Important: After rubbing and circling, be sure you finish with a few glides up the shoulder, toward the head. Use four fingers or palms for these glides. Add these upward glides because you want to flush the toxins from this area.

No Thanks _____   My Dog Likes _____   My Dog Really Likes _____

Back for More

The back is a great area to massage! Even on a small dog there's so much area to cover. And for big burly dogs, there's unlimited choices. Enjoy the full range of *everything* here—use all hand parts, positions, motions, pressures, and speeds to create all the different moods. Learning good back work is essential for satisfying massage sessions. Strokes can get wider, and with more area to cover, we see full gliding, strumming, and ruffling. Speeds can get faster, pressures deeper, and the mood swings are welcomed here, from gentle and relaxed to playful to frolicky fun. Enjoy!

Back strokes are among the easiest to learn. They provide good practice that builds courage and confidence for more detailed work. Expert massage here will keep your dog coming Back for More.

With the lower back area, some dogs flinch at first contact, so approach cautiously. Or if Dog is totally not interested, leave the area alone. There's plenty of other areas to massage.

Never press directly on spine.

CAUTION

Back Techniques

1. The Grand *Effleurage*
2. Hand Over Hand and Down We Go: A Two-Handed Double Delight
3. Base Fiddling
4. Ruffling Shuffle
5. Back Horseshoes
6. Spine Tingling
7. Finger Padding Along the Vertebrae
8. Gentle Rump Thumping
9. Farewell Flourishes

The Grand *Effleurage*

Pronounced "Eff-loor-**ahj**"—the French term for stroking.

AREA: Entire length of the back (and neck) and the broad sides of the Dog.

HAND PARTS: Closed palms, open palms, four fingers, two fingers, finger pads, fingertips.

HAND POSITIONS: Cupping, horizontal, vertical, palm down.

MOTION: Gliding.

SPEEDS: Slow-mo, leisurely, fast 'n' frisky.

PRESSURES: Mild, light, featherlight, deep with Dog's approval.

MOODS: Gentle and relaxed, playful, frolicky fun.

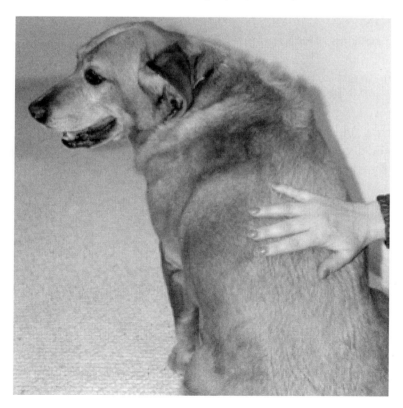

An entire Dog Massage session can be built around this major technique, and soon you'll know why. It's the master stroke of Dog Massage.

TECHNIQUE:

Start high up between the ears. With closed palm, glide your hand all the way down the length of Dog's back. Then continue right to the tip of the tail. Don't stop at mid or low back. It's like half a handshake. Repeat at least three or four times for familiarity. Now get creative and playful with this technique. First experiment with speed. Count how many seconds it takes for you to do a full stroke. Then *double* that time. Time yourself for accuracy, because it's hard to go so slowly. Your dog will enjoy the extended caress. Remember the definition of slow-mo: What seems excruciatingly slow for you can feel very appropriate to your dog. The slow motion of this stroke allows *you* to establish a pace, and *Dog* to acknowledge, accept, approve, and appreciate your touch. It's well worth the effort. Alternate speeds, right up to fast 'n' frisky.

Now use open palms, and then repeat with four fingers and two fingers. Alternate with finger pads. Run them along his back, and then bend your fingers and allow the fingertips to glide along. If yours is a larger dog, you may want to stick with palms. And if yours is smaller, fingers may be all you need for coverage.

Vary pressures. Start with mild pressure, what you're probably most comfortable and familiar with. Then deliberately change your pressure to light for a few strokes. Now for an interesting chance of pace, go featherlight. This is particularly interesting on very large breeds, like a Great Dane or a Norwegian elkhound. Large dogs are not likely to be accustomed to such a featherlight touch. Watch their response. Which does Dog prefer? Which do you prefer? Is there a common pressure you both prefer?

Pay attention to the bony landmarks and borders of the back. Watch your hand move as it crosses the bony shoulder blades. This technique allows for the most flexibility of all strokes, so take advantage of it. Explore your range of options to discover the true beauty of this technique. You'll see and feel how The Grand *Effleurage* can be gentle and relaxed, playful, and frolicky fun.

VARIATION:

Start with one hand. When you're comfortable, coordinate with two and repeat the techniques. The back wants full coverage.

No Thanks _____   My Dog Likes _____   My Dog Really Likes _____

Hand Over Hand and Down We Go:
A Two-Handed Double Delight

AREA: Back (and neck).

HAND PARTS: Open palms, knuckle nooks, four fingers, closed palms.

HAND POSITIONS: Horizontal, vertical, horseshoe, cupping, palm down.

MOTION: Gliding.

SPEEDS: Slow-mo, leisurely, fast 'n' frisky.

PRESSURES: Light, medium, deep with Dog's approval.

MOODS: Gentle and relaxed, playful, frolicky fun.

TECHNIQUE:

Starting at the top of her head, glide one hand (either right or left) down your dog's back. When your hand is halfway down,

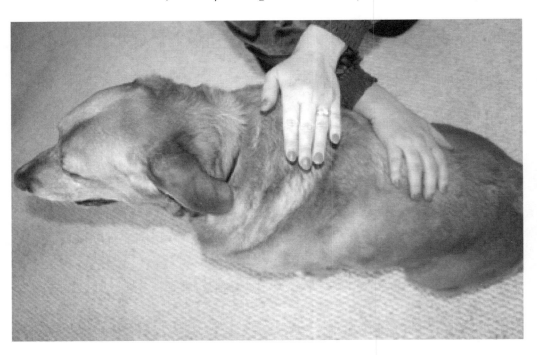

start your other hand at the top, and begin that hand on its downward glide. As your first hand approaches the low back, glide it off, and continue again from the top. Repeat with your other hand, so you create a wide, continuous loop between your two hands and Dog's back. Continue this in a coordinated motion (which may take a bit of practice) and find a comfortable rhythm.

Some of these two-handed strokes can be long and flowing, with one glide covering the entire length of the back. Others can be shorter moves, with three glides to cover the back. Make them even smaller, and you'll fit six glides along her back. Think of maintaining a flowing, cascading motion. The two-handed approach makes this another marvelous technique. Practice before you build up speed. For continuity, keep at least one hand on Dog at all times.

Just as with The Grand *Effleurage,* explore all hand parts, hand positions, motions, pressures, speeds, and moods. Have fun!

No Thanks _____   My Dog Likes _____   My Dog Really Likes _____

Base Fiddling

AREA: The lowest part of Dog's back—the rump.

HAND PARTS: Open palm, closed palm, four fingers, two fingers.

HAND POSITIONS: Horizontal, palm down.

MOTION: Waving.

SPEEDS: Slow-mo, leisurely, fast 'n' frisky.

PRESSURES: Light, mild, deep with Dog's approval.

MOODS: Gentle and relaxed, playful, fast 'n' frisky.

TECHNIQUE:

With a downward horizontal waving motion, stroke back and forth along the lowest third of Dog's back, about two to three inches above the base of the tail.

Use your palms (open or closed) or the flat part of your fingers. Repeat this ruffle back and forth a few times, just covering the few inches above the tail base.

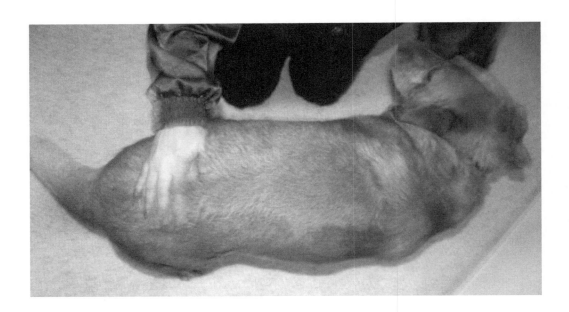

Concentrate on smooth repetition, and adjust your pressure, speed, and mood in response to Dog's feedback. Keep your strokes short while covering this area.

Often there's a slight slapping sound as your pinkie finger slaps against the tail itself. Some dogs enjoy deep pressure at this point—so much so that it will almost seem as if their legs are going to collapse under the weight of your hands.

Dogs who enjoy this technique may actually rub back against you in delight. There are some dogs who simply do not enjoy this technique at all. If so, move on to another one.

The lumbosacral junction is a common site for disc disease. Your dog might object to massage in this area because of pain. If that's the case, discuss it with your veterinarian. If your dog suddenly displays sensitivity here, also consult your vet.

CAUTION

No Thanks _____   My Dog Likes _____   My Dog Really Likes _____

Ruffling Shuffle

AREA: Back.

HAND PARTS: Open palm, closed palm, four fingers, finger-tips, finger pads.

HAND POSITIONS: Horizontal, vertical, palm down.

MOTIONS: Waving, rubbing.

SPEEDS: Slow-mo, leisurely, fast 'n' frisky.

PRESSURES: Light, mild, deep with Dog's approval.

MOODS: Gentle and relaxed, playful, frolicky fun.

TECHNIQUE:

With palm (open or closed) or fingers, begin at the base of the neck, using a downward and horizontal ruffling wave for the first third of the back. Without stopping, reverse direction and stroke back up to your starting point, rubbing gently against the fur. Stroke further down again, and then back up, again and again. Keep this waving a fluid motion, gently flowing up and down the entire back.

Repeat the stroke vertically, starting with your palms and fingers at the base of the neck. Now like a windshield wiper, ruffle some more. Repeat with a ruffling motion. Keep a gentle rocking motion, and allow your dog to enjoy your artistry. Afterward, make sure to unruffle the ruffled fur with hand, brush, or comb.

Dogs with very short hair may be extremely sensitive to having their fur ruffled. Others may simply resent their coat being disturbed. In either case, respect this and move on to another technique.

CAUTION

No Thanks _____   My Dog Likes _____   My Dog Really Likes _____

Back Horseshoes

AREA: Back.
HAND PARTS: Closed palm, four fingers.
HAND POSITIONS: Horizontal, horseshoe.
MOTION: Gliding.
SPEED: Slow-mo.
PRESSURES: Light, mild.
MOOD: Gentle and relaxed.

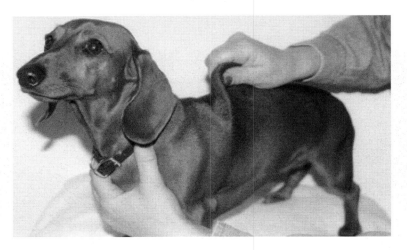

TECHNIQUE:

This will be a dip, squeeze, pull-up, release motion. In a horizontal horseshoe position (upside-down letter ∪), put closed palm on Dog's back, by her shoulders. Add a slight squeeze as you slowly glide your four fingers up. At the end of the pull-up, release pressure. Be careful to not pinch the fur. Reach down again, grasp some fur, and again, slowly pull up. Then move your hand further down along the spine and continue this action as you move toward the tail.

ADVANCED TECHNIQUE:

Still in the horseshoe position, with a long gliding motion, slide your hand along the spine from neck to rump. Then return up. Repeat a few times. Remember that return strokes always have light pressures.

Never press or squeeze too deeply.

CAUTION

No Thanks _____   My Dog Likes _____   My Dog Really Likes _____

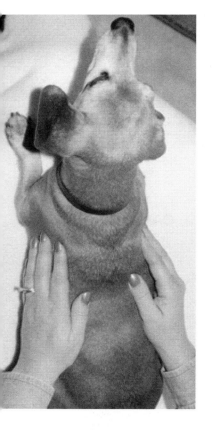

Spine Tingling

AREA: Back, from neck to rump.
HAND PARTS: Finger pads, thumb pads.
HAND POSITIONS: Palm down, vertical.
MOTION: Rubbing.
PRESSURES: Light, mild, deep with Dog's approval.
SPEEDS: Slow-mo, leisurely.
MOODS: Gentle and relaxed, playful.

TECHNIQUE:

Position finger pads on either side of the spine, resting the pinkie part of your palm on Dog's body. Slowly rub your thumb pads in a twiddling motion over a small area, with the spine in between them. Cover only about an inch or so. Gauge Dog's response, and if favorable, continue a bit further up, then a bit further down. Repeat down the spine until you've reached the tail, and work your way back up the same way.

VARIATION:

Position both hands along the outside of the spine, pinkie part of the palms resting on Dog.

Twiddle both thumb pads along the left side of the spine, and twiddle both thumb pads along the right side of the spine.

CAUTION

If your dog doesn't like her fur ruffled, continue to another technique.

No Thanks _____　My Dog Likes _____　My Dog Really Likes _____

Finger Padding Along the Vertebrae

AREA: Ridges along either side of the spine.
HAND PART: Finger pads.
HAND POSITION: Horizontal.
MOTIONS: Circling, flicking.
PRESSURES: Light, mild, deep with approval.
SPEEDS: Slow-mo, leisurely.
MOOD: Gentle and relaxed.

Note: this is *not* a technique for long fingernails.

TECHNIQUE:

Using finger pads, feel the ridges on one side of the spine. Keep to the side, not the top. Rest one, two, three, or even four finger pads in the area. You'll feel the bumpy parts of the vertebrae called the transverse processes.

Make very tiny circles, about the size of a dime. These circles are so small that you'll be barely moving your finger pads. The circling becomes almost a vibrating motion. Make them slightly

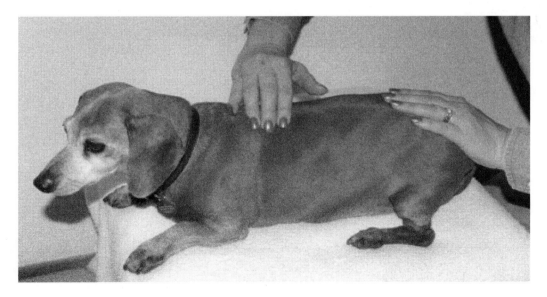

larger, keeping them along the grooves at the side of the spine. Sink into the area, feeling the muscles, tendons, and ligaments located there. Get familiar, and remember to circle counter-clockwise. Start from as high up along the back as you can, and continue as far down to the rump as you can. The shape and size of your dog and your dog's feedback will determine how many finger pads you can use, and how far and deep you can work.

Work very slowly. It is more important to sink in and loosen up a muscle than it is to cover distance. Remember to work both sides equally.

VARIATION:

Like tapping your fingers on a table, do this along sides of the spine with your finger pads.

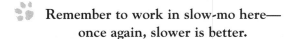 **Remember to work in slow-mo here—
once again, slower is better.**

Adjust your pressure with Dog. She may enjoy light, tolerate mild, and even request deep. As always, follow her feedback.

VARIATION:

Use a flicking motion. Like pressing down on a pump dispenser, do this along the spine. Adjust pressure to your dog's preferences, and again, go for the slow, in a gentle and relaxed mood.

**Working along the spine is a great way to
relax the muscles that all connect, in some way, to the
backbone of your dog.**

No Thanks _____   My Dog Likes _____   My Dog Really Likes _____

Gentle Rump Thumping

AREA: Base of the spine.
HAND PARTS: Two fingers, thenar eminence, closed palm,
   four fingers, open palm.
HAND POSITIONS: Cupping, palm down.
MOTION: Rubbing.
PRESSURES: Featherlight, light, mild, deep.
SPEEDS: Slow-mo, leisurely, fast 'n' frisky.
MOODS: Gentle and relaxed, playful, frolicky fun.

Upgrade the familiar patting the dog with your new hand
parts, pressures, and speeds.

TECHNIQUE:

Position your hand near the base of Dog's tail, and gently pat.
Use the different hand parts listed and cover the entire rump.
Feel the difference between gentle rump thumping with two fin-
gers, with the thenar eminence, or with a closed palm. Four fin-

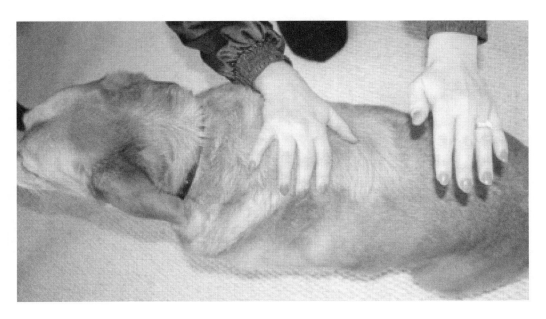

gers may be enough for smaller dogs, while larger breeds may enjoy full open palms patting away.

You can offer choices in pressures, and your dog will help you decide which to use. Some prefer lighter pressures and others deeper, so follow your dog's feedback. Alternate all the speeds, too. See how different combinations create all the different moods.

VARIATION:

At the end of the pat, add a small rub. The motion will be straight down, then a slight curve, like you're forming the letter J.

Never go too deep. Follow your dog's guidance.

No Thanks _____   My Dog Likes _____   My Dog Really Likes _____

Farewell Flourishes

AREA: Back.

HAND PARTS: Finger pads, fingertips, four fingers, palms (open and closed).

HAND POSITIONS: Horizontal or vertical, palm down.

MOTION: Gliding.

SPEEDS: Slow-mo, leisurely.

PRESSURES: Featherlight, light, mild.

MOOD: Gentle and relaxed.

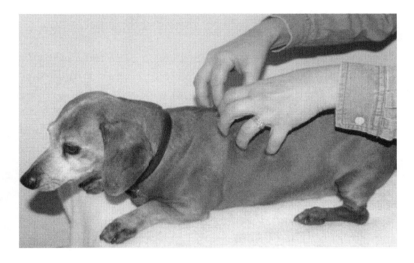

TECHNIQUE:

Keep the speed slow-mo to leisurely. Start pressure with featherlight and build up to mild. Keep mood gentle and relaxed. Use gracious, glorious gliding motions (employing all the hand parts and positions listed) that cascade along your dog's back. Make your technique smooth and calm, not rapid. Do this in groups of three glides at a time. And be sure to continue out to the tip of the tail. This signals the end of a massage. Short and sweet, another simple and successful stroke. A flourishing finale to every Dog Massage.

No Thanks _____   My Dog Likes _____   My Dog Really Likes _____

Let's Do a Little Necking

Dogs get neck pains, aches, or just plain muscle fatigue, just as people do. Dogs' necks are involved in almost everything they do: craning their heads to look out of windows, sleeping curled up for long periods of times, darting their heads back and forth to watch a moth, or just lifting their heads to observe a world that is mostly above them. Many dogs prefer the neck as a favorite area for massage because it feels so good.

The dog's neck (top side) is supported by the first seven vertebrae of the spine. These bones are called the cervical vertebrae. At the top end, they attach directly to the dog's skull. At the lower end, they continue into the thoracic vertebrae, near the shoulder blades. Feel around there on your dog. The bumps you feel directly on the dog's spine are called the spinous processes. Each vertebra also has a bony protuberance on each side called the transverse process.

There's so much activity within the neck area, with a multitude of muscles, bones, tendons, nerves, and blood vessels involved. Relaxing massage work in this area has a soothing effect that your dog will feel all over.

A very important point to remember here is that you *never* press directly onto the spine, since it is a very delicate structure. You never want to be or give a pain in the neck to your canine friend. Appropriate massage work in and around the neck may

be very welcome here. Because this is a small area, many techniques can be worked either horizontally or vertically for more
variety. The dog's neck, just like your neck, enjoys massage. So
collect your dog, find a comfortable place, and let's do a little
necking.

Neck Techniques

1. Classic Pet: A Fido Favorite
2. Waving Down the Neckline
3. Cross-Neck Flicking
4. Occipital Bump Rubbing
5. Neck Horseshoes

Classic Pet: A Fido Favorite

AREA: Top and sides of the neck.

HAND PARTS: Finger pads, palms (open or closed), four fingers, thenar eminence, knuckle nooks, fingertips, two fingers, finger sides, thumb, thumb pad.

HAND POSITIONS: Vertical, horizontal, cupping.

MOTIONS: Gliding, rubbing.

SPEEDS: Slow-mo, leisurely, fast 'n' frisky.

PRESSURES: Light, featherlight, mild, deep.

MOODS: Gentle and relaxed, playful, frolicky fun.

This is already a familiar touch. Most of us instinctively rub a dog at the top of the neck, between the ears. Now let's upgrade it to a massage technique.

TECHNIQUE:

Position your hand in the vertical position, parallel to your dog's spine. Glide lightly from neck to shoulders, with pressure on the down stroke only. Start with finger pads, palms (open or

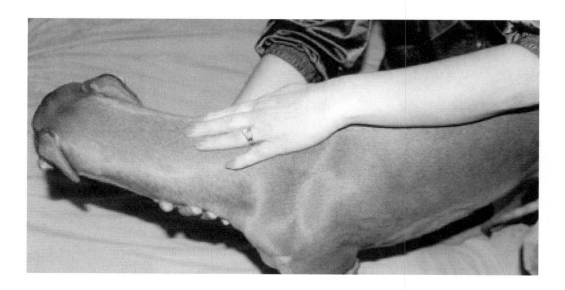

closed), or four fingers together. Alternate all your hand parts, just like you did with the shoulder and back. Stroke the neck with the thenar eminence, then with knuckle nooks, and continue down the list. Which hand part does your dog prefer? Which do you prefer?

Now vary your hand positions. Start with your hand vertical and parallel to the neck; then change it to a horizontal position, with your hand perpendicular to the spine. Alternate that with cupping, so your hand covers both the top and the sides of the neck.

Begin with gliding motions, then short rubbing back and forth. Add some slow strumming, as your fingertips gently caress Dog's coat. Cover the tops and sides of the neck. Some dogs will press their neck up to match your hand pressure.

Pressures will vary with your dog's desires. Start, as always, with a light pressure. Work featherlightly and watch Dog's response. Then proceed to mild, and with Dog's approval, work deep.

Start with slow-mo, and pay attention to the speed variations. Some dogs like a leisurely pace here, and others will prefer fast 'n' frisky. Follow your canine's critiques for best results.

VARIATION:

Add in a light pressure rippling motion, like playing the flute. Begin with the pinkie and end with the thumb.

No Thanks _____   My Dog Likes _____   My Dog Really Likes _____

Waving Down the Neckline

AREA: Top and sides of neck.
HAND PARTS: Finger pads, knuckle nooks, thenar eminence, four fingers, open palms, closed palms, two fingers, thumb pads.
HAND POSITION: Vertical.
MOTION: Waving.
SPEEDS: Slow-mo, leisurely, fast 'n' frisky.
PRESSURES: Featherlight, light, mild, deep.
MOODS: Gentle and relaxed, playful, frolicky fun.

TECHNIQUE:

With your fingers in the vertical position, wave sideways like a windshield wiper, or waving good-bye. Work your way down along the neck. Alternate short, half-inch waves with longer waves, using all of the hand parts listed. Allow gentle waves to extend along the sides of Dog's neck, too, with as much pressure as she allows. Alternate pressures and speeds, following your dog's responses.

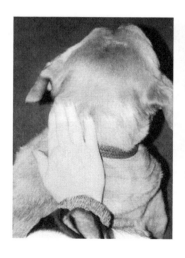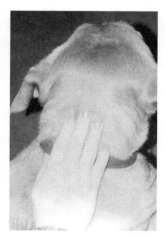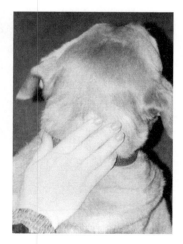

CAUTION: Be aware of the weight of your hand, especially for small dogs. Be careful not to unintentionally shove her head forward during this technique.

CAUTION

🐾 **Do this properly, and your dog will be waving to *you* as soon as you're in sight.**

No Thanks _____   My Dog Likes _____   My Dog Really Likes _____

Cross-Neck Flicking

AREA: Neck.
HAND PART: Fingertips.
HAND POSITION: Horizontal.
MOTION: Flicking.
SPEEDS: Slow-mo, leisurely.
PRESSURES: Featherlight, light, mild.
MOODS: Gentle and relaxed, playful.

CAUTION

Long fingernails must work with lighter pressures, because this is a delicate area.

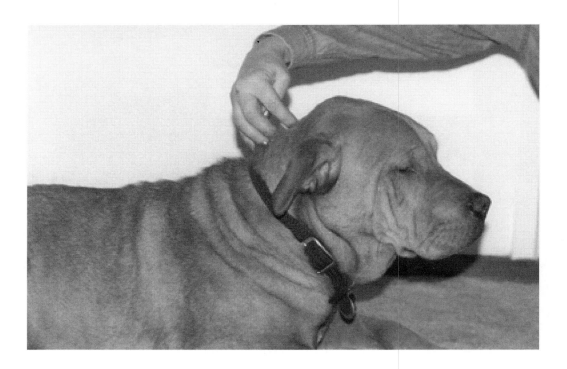

TECHNIQUE:

With a flicking motion, stroke Dog's neck. Work back and forth across the spine, moving up and down the length of the neck, using your fingertips. Flick along one side of the neck, then on top. Work featherlightly when working over the vertebrae. Move to the other side of the neck and flick some more. Flick with different pressure and speeds. Slow, deep flicking generates a different response than light, fast flicking. Which does your dog prefer?

Be careful to not push the neck forward during this technique.

CAUTION

No Thanks _____   My Dog Likes _____   My Dog Really Likes _____

Occipital Bump Rubbing

AREA: Occiput, the bump at the back of the dog's head.
HAND PARTS: Finger pads, fingertips, four fingers, two fingers.
HAND POSITIONS: Horizontal, vertical, cupping.
MOTIONS: Circling, waving, rubbing.
SPEEDS: Slow-mo, leisurely, fast 'n' frisky.
PRESSURES: Featherlight, light, mild, deep.
MOODS: Gentle and relaxed, playful.

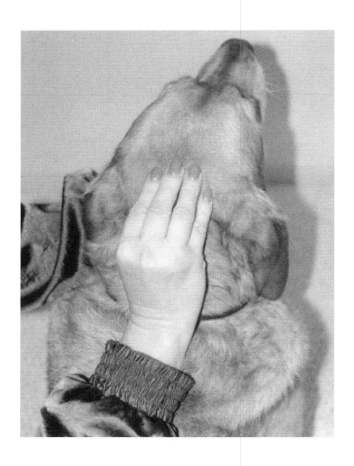

TECHNIQUE:

Locate the bump at the back of your dog's head, which is called the occiput. Massage this bump with one or more finger pads rotating in tiny circles. Try fingertips for a precise feel. Then use four fingers for a broad approach. Next, position your index and middle fingers so that the occiput is between them, and gently wave back and forth. And of course, you can cover the area with small rubbing motions. Alternate the speed and pressure according to Dog's critique.

No flicking here, because the area is bony, not soft.

CAUTION

VARIATION:

As you massage the occiput with one hand, cup the chin in the other hand. This allows for more area to be explored, and Dog is more comfortable, having her head supported.

No Thanks _____   My Dog Likes _____   My Dog Really Likes _____

Neck Horseshoes

AREA: Neck.
HAND PARTS: Closed palm, four fingers, thumb.
HAND POSITIONS: Horizontal, horseshoe.
MOTION: Gliding.
SPEEDS: Slow-mo, leisurely.
PRESSURES: Light, mild, can get deep.
MOODS: Gentle and relaxed, playful.

TECHNIQUE:

Just like Back Horseshoes, this is a dip, squeeze, pull-up, release motion. In a horizontal horseshoe position (upside-down letter U), put closed palm on dog's neck. Your thumb will be resting on the side of her neck, the web of your hand across her spine, and your four fingers on the other side of the neck. With a light squeeze, slowly glide your hand up. At the end of the pull-up, release pressure. Be careful not to pinch the fur. Reach down again, grasp some fur, lightly squeeze, and slowly pull up. Repeat a few times along the neck area. Follow Dog's feedback for approval.

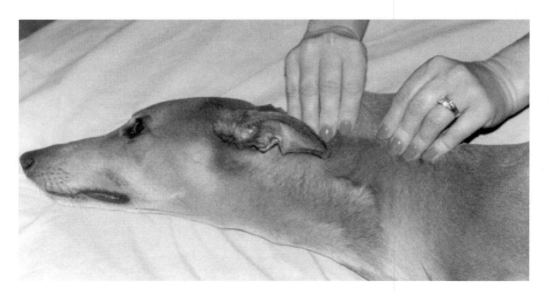

For best results, go for the slow.

This can be a very soothing, relaxing technique. Adjust your pressures according to Dog's responses. If your dog has a furry coat, you may grasp a good bit of fur. If yours is a shorthaired canine, there will be less fur available, so be careful not to squeeze too hard.

Squeeze lightly, gently, never aggressively.

CAUTION

No Thanks _____   My Dog Likes _____   My Dog Really Likes _____

Getting Into It Head First

The head is an ideal place for Dog Massage, so let's take it from the top. By now, you will have become familiar with your particular canine's critiques. From the friendly and unfriendly feedback, you'll have a good sense of his likes and dislikes, and how he expresses them.

 Noticing and responding to Unfriendly Feedback is especially important in this sensitive area.

Your dog has probably already invited you to Dog Massage by stretching his head to meet your extended hand. The head is an exceptionally sensitive area, especially the face, because all the sense organs are located here: the eyes, nose, mouth, whiskers, and ears. Therefore, *you* need to be particularly sensitive here, especially with long fingernails. Keep massage motions slow and consistent in pressure and speed. Listen and watch closely.

Most dogs like their heads worked on because it's difficult for them to groom and clean this area. They may enjoy you touching it for them. Precise, slow detailed head work can intensify the bond between you and your canine companion.

Head tips: Depending on the size of your dog, the head area may be very small and sensitive. In that case, massage strokes here will be shorter movements and slower speeds. Bigger dogs may enjoy deeper work—again, always pay attention to Dog's responses.

Once again, this is a most sensitive area. Do not attempt these techniques if your dog is mouthy. Mouthy means the dog has a tendency to put his mouth on your wrist, hand, or fingers. Work on his shoulders, back, and neck; get familiar with your dog's dislikes and pleasures before working here.

CAUTION

Head Techniques

1. Chin-Ups
2. Crowning the King/Queen
3. Check Out Those Cheeks: A Facial Favorite
4. Apex Flicking
5. Ear Nooking: aka Trace the Ear Base
6. Smoothing Over the Whisker Beds
7. Thenar Bucca Buffing
8. Emily's Forehead Favorite
9. Side of the Head Stroking

Chin-Ups

AREA: The entire triangular chin area, from the back of the throat to the tip of the chin.

HAND PARTS: Finger pads, fingertips, finger sides, two fingers, four fingers, open palm, closed palm, thumb, thenar eminence.

HAND POSITIONS: Palm up, palm down, cupping, horizontal, horseshoe, vertical.

MOTIONS: Rubbing, circling, flicking, gliding, waving.

SPEEDS: Slow-mo, leisurely, no-mo (interesting touch).

PRESSURES: Featherlight, light.

MOODS: Gentle and relaxed, playful.

🐾 **Be careful of the windpipe here,
especially if you use a vertical approach.**

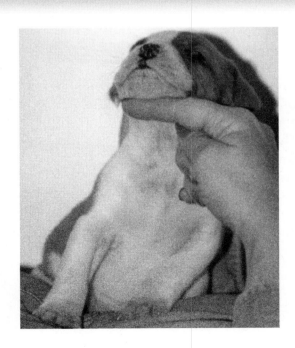

Starting head work under the chin is effective because in this position, the dog is on top of all the action. Dog feels secure to have his eyes, ears, and nose on top of your hand.

TECHNIQUE:

Use finger pads to stroke under the chin. Start in slow-mo, don't go faster than leisurely. Start with little rubs back and forth. Lightly massage from the throat out to the tip of the chin. Next do some circling, small dime-sized shapes, barely moving your hand at all. Make them larger, quarter-sized shapes. When you're comfortable, and with Dog approval, alternate with other hand parts and the other motions.

 **The clearest indication of technique approval is for Dog to crane his head up, chin pointing up toward the sky. This is a purely positive Rover response. When it happens, you'll know you're right on target!**

VARIATION—CHIN CUPPING:

Now cup your hand and use your open palm to caress the area. From the throat out to the chin, and side to side—cup on!

ADVANCED TECHNIQUE—NO-MO CUPPING:

This is surprisingly relaxing, where no action is most effective. Using closed palm, cup Dog's head in your hand, and let it rest there, not moving at all. This feels good for Dog to have the weight of his head supported in your hand. Or rest his head on your lap. Try it—it's contrary to our human nature of always doing something, but it's quite comfortable for our canine companions.

Note: Always watch for and respond to any unfriendly feedback.

ADVANCED VARIATION—GENTLE SQUEEZE CUPPING:

Add a gentle squeeze to the area. Do two squeezes per second. Count to yourself, "One, one thousand, two, one thousand." By then you will have four squeezes. Go for the slow and go even slower.

VARIATION—FOUR-FINGER CHIN REST:

Position your hand, palm down, with four fingers together and bent. Your fingers can rest under Dog's throat, your knuckle nooks under her chin. Let your hand become a resting post for Dog's chin. Simply allow Dog to rest on it—a no-mo technique that many dogs love!

See all the possibilities? Use simple adjustments and you'll have plenty to keep you and your canine companion happily busy.

No Thanks _____   My Dog Likes _____   My Dog Really Likes _____

Crowning the King/Queen

AREA: Top of the head—from forehead to back of neck; side to side—from ear to ear.
HAND PARTS: Finger pads, fingertips, knuckle nooks.
HAND POSITION: Palm down.
MOTIONS: Circling, rubbing.
SPEEDS: Slow-mo, leisurely.
PRESSURES: Featherlight, light, mild, deep on approval.
MOODS: Gentle and relaxed, playful.

TECHNIQUE:

With finger pads and fingertips, pattern circles on top of Dog's head. Or use your knuckle nooks. Make small circles the size of a silver dollar, and cover the boundaries of the forehead, ears, and neck. Then make tiny circles, dime-sized, with your fingers pads barely moving at all. Alternate with larger circles, wide enough to cover the entire top of his head. Or just do short rubs. Vary your pressures. The featherlight movements will barely make surface contact with fur. The light and mild pressures allow you to feel the bony parts of the head and neck. Vary speeds. Start slow-mo, and experiment, always following your dog's responses. Does Dog prefer clockwise or counter-clockwise? Soon Dog may be moving his head in response to your fingers. Perhaps he'll close his eyes and sigh in contented response.

Try this technique with all the different hand parts.

No Thanks _____   My Dog Likes _____   My Dog Really Likes _____

Check Out Those Cheeks:
A Facial Favorite

AREA: Cheek, in front of the ear line—up to the whiskers.

HAND PARTS: Finger pads, thenar eminence, knuckles, knuckle nooks, fingertips, finger sides, four fingers, two fingers, thumb pad.

HAND POSITION: Horizontal.

MOTIONS: Circling, rubbing.

SPEED: Slow-mo.

PRESSURES: Light, mild, featherlight.

MOODS: Gentle and relaxed, playful.

TECHNIQUE:

With finger pads, caress the cheek area slowly and carefully. Tenderly massage circles with light and mild pressures. Make them counterclockwise, too. Then alternate circles with short rubs, back and forth. Now, try this same technique with different hand parts. Stroke with each hand part at least five times, or for ten seconds. This gives Dog a chance to express his preferences. It also encourages *you* to slow down.

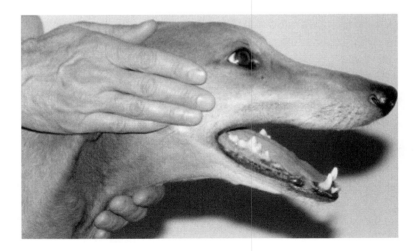

VARIATION:

For an interesting change of pace, work featherlight. Feel only for the fur. Because this is a sensitive area, Dog may prefer exceptionally light pressure.

A Whisker Watch Alert is in effect here. If you touch near the whiskers, remember how sensitive they are—so be careful not to bend them forward.

CAUTION

The cheek teeth, in particular the largest tooth on top and furthest back, is a common place for dental disease. If such a condition is present, it could make any touching in this area uncomfortable or painful. Avoid this area and consult your veterinarian.

CAUTION

No Thanks _____   My Dog Likes _____   My Dog Really Likes _____

Apex Flicking

AREA: The top of the head—from the highest point to the neck.
HAND PART: Fingertips.
HAND POSITION: Palm down.
MOTION: Flicking.
SPEEDS: Slow-mo, leisurely.
PRESSURES: Featherlight, light, mild.
MOODS: Gentle and relaxed, playful.

TECHNIQUE:

First, practice a few flicking motions from Tools of the Trade (page 35). This motion is similar to flicking crumbs off a table or pressing down on a pump dispenser. Begin gentle fingertip flicking motions across the top of the head. Use the index finger, middle finger or both. Follow to the base of each ear and back to center.

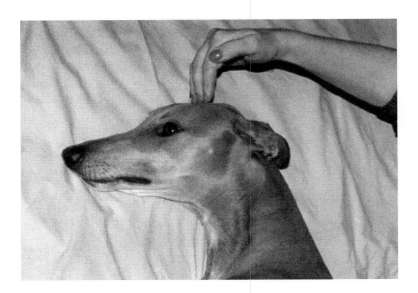

Shorthaired dogs may find this too intense for comfort. If so, stop massage, and proceed to another technique. Be careful with longer fingernails, especially around the ears.

CAUTION

No Thanks _____   My Dog Likes _____   My Dog Really Likes _____

Ear Nooking: aka Trace the Ear Base

AREA: Base of dog's ear.
HAND PARTS: Knuckle nooks, two fingers.
HAND POSITION: Palm down.
MOTIONS: Circling, rubbing.
SPEEDS: Slo-mo, leisurely.
PRESSURES: Featherlight, light, mild.
MOOD: Gentle and relaxed.

TECHNIQUE:

Using your knuckle nooks, slowly trace tiny clockwise circles below the base of Dog's ear. This is the area directly below the ear opening and on both sides—not the opening itself. Perhaps Dog will twist and rotate her head against your hand in delightful response.

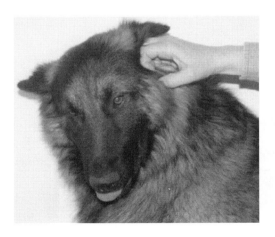 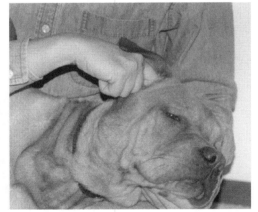

The ear is highly sensitive, so keep the mood gentle and relaxed and speeds slow. Watch your pressures.

CAUTION

VARIATION:

Some dogs encourage light massaging of the ear itself. Slowly caress the ear with the index and middle fingers together, the ear in the middle, and the thumb below. Rub carefully and slowly.

It is not uncommon for a dog to have a mild ear infection without your being aware of it. This could make that technique painful for your dog. If your dog reacts unfavorably, especially if this has been a preferred technique in the past, consult your vet.

CAUTION

No Thanks _____   My Dog Likes _____   My Dog Really Likes _____

Smoothing Over the Whisker Beds

AREA: Whisker beds.
HAND PARTS: Finger pads, thumbs, two fingers, four fingers.
MOTION: Rubbing.
SPEED: Slow-mo.
PRESSURES: Light, mild.
MOOD: Gentle and relaxed.

TECHNIQUE:

The whisker beds are the base of the whiskers where they attach to Dog's cheek.

There may be increased sensitivity on Dog's part. If he is not interested in this technique, proceed to the next one. Wait until you've worked on the head for a few minutes and warmed up the area before Smoothing Over the Whisker Beds. Be sure you are aware of your canine's critiques in this area. Respond to any Unfriendly Feedback by stopping your massage. Ever so slowly, start at the tip of Dog's nose. Slowly rub over the whiskers and the whisker beds. Do not massage the actual whiskers, and don't

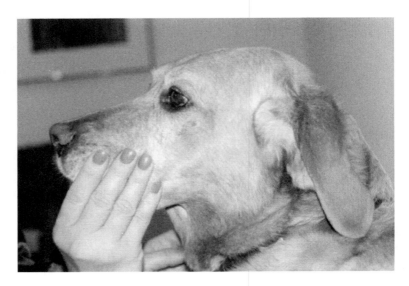

back up over them. Continue your caress along the side of the head back to the cheek area. Keep your pressure light or mild. Featherlight may be too light and cause an uncomfortable tickling. Important: Go for the Slow.

A major Whisker Watch Alert is in effect here. No touching and no bending them. Be very patient and very careful here because everything is so sensitive.

CAUTION

Sudden work in this area can startle a dog, so *be very careful*. This specific area generally doesn't receive much touch. However, when done properly, this technique feels so good.

No Thanks _____   My Dog Likes _____   My Dog Really Likes _____

Thenar Bucca Buffing

AREA: Dog cheeks (*buccae*), behind the whiskers, closer to the back of the head.

HAND PART: Thenar eminence, thumb pads.

HAND POSITION: Vertical.

MOTIONS: Rubbing, circling.

SPEEDS: Slow-mo, no-mo.

PRESSURES: Light, mild.

MOOD: Gentle and relaxed.

TECHNIQUE:

The thenar eminence is simply the fleshy part of the palm below the thumb. Thenar bucca buffing is a fancy name for the coordi-

nated rubbing of your thenar eminence along your dog's cheeks (*buccae*). It's a bit tricky to understand, but truly welcomed. Hold your palm out on one side of Dog's head. Rest your thenar eminence against his cheek, behind the whiskers. Start with a few short rubs back across her cheek, from front to back. Now start circling—clockwise. Get comfortable, and start counterclockwise—at least six times to get the feel of it. See if Dog rubs back in response. Keep your pressures light and mild, and your speed slow.

VARIATION:

Use two hands to coordinate thenar eminence–cheek action. Use thumb pads.

VARIATION:

Enjoy a two-handed no-mo moment. Position both thenar eminences along both sides of Dog's head. Just let Dog's head rest within your hands. Be still together for a few moments and enjoy the inactivity.

ADVANCED VARIATION:

Rub circles in unison, slowly caressing Dog's cheeks. Then alternate the circles. While the right palm is at the top of the circle on one side of the cheek, the left palm is at the bottom of the circle on the side of the other cheek.

A Whisker Watch Alert is in effect here. Stay behind them, closer to the ear, and be careful not to bend them forward.

CAUTION

No Thanks _____   My Dog Likes _____   My Dog Really Likes _____

Emily's Forehead Favorite

AREA: Forehead—the inverted triangle between the ears down to the tip of the nose.

HAND PARTS: Finger pads, thenar eminence, fingertips, four fingers, two fingers, knuckle nooks, thumb pads, finger sides, closed palm, knuckles.

HAND POSITIONS: Horizontal, palm down.

MOTIONS: Rubbing, circling, waving.

SPEEDS: Slow-mo, leisurely.

PRESSURES: Featherlight, light, mild.

MOODS: Gentle and relaxed, playful.

TECHNIQUE:

With two or four fingers in a horizontal position, rub your fingers up and down Dog's forehead. (Eventually, try all the hand parts listed.) Next use a waving motion and caress across the forehead. Then make circles. From the tip of the nose to the top of your dog's head—he'll show you where to massage.

VARIATION:

When using four fingers, lift one or two fingers, then replace them and lift different fingers—like very featherlight piano playing.

No Thanks _____   My Dog Likes _____   My Dog Really Likes _____

CAUTION   **Be careful of Dog's eyes.**

Side of the Head Stroking

AREA: Side of the head, behind and under the ear line.
HAND PARTS: Knuckles, knuckle nooks, four fingers, thenar eminence, finger pads, fingertips, closed palm, open palm.
HAND POSITIONS: Cupping, horizontal, vertical.
MOTIONS: Waving, circling, flicking, rubbing, gliding.
SPEEDS: Slow-mo, leisurely, fast 'n' frisky.
PRESSURES: Light, mild, can go deep with approval.
MOODS: Gentle and relaxed, playful.

TECHNIQUE:

Using all the hand parts listed, caress the side part of Dog's head, behind and under the ear line. Depending on the size of your dog, use all motions. Wave up and down and side to side. Circle to the left, circle to the right. Slowly glide and strum in this area. Hold your palm against the neck, and flick all four fingers in unison. If your dog is fleshy in that area, grasp onto some skin with a slight squeeze and pull action. This is a major response area. Enjoy the feedback.

No Thanks _____   My Dog Likes _____   My Dog Really Likes _____

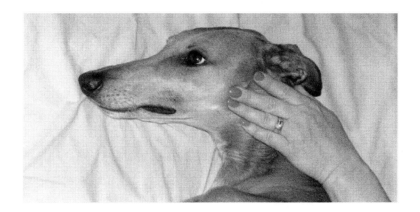

Side Stroking

Bring to mind the image of a dog relaxing, and it will often be that of a dog reclining on its side. Lying on one side exposes quite a large amount of body surface area, and invites a multitude of mellow massage work, especially long, luxurious stroking.

Now that our capable hands have learned strokes for the head, neck, and shoulders of our favorite canine, it's only a matter of time before we massage the sides of their bodies as well. Movements here are very gentle and relaxed, and Side Stroking is often a prelude to Tummy Touching. Many dogs that start their massage standing or sitting will often finish reclining on their side.

Side Techniques

1. Light Fur Fluffing: A Subtle, Satisfying Stroke
2. Dog Sandwich
3. Layla's Luxurious Front-to-Back Caress
4. Alternating Circular Side Waving
5. Side Palming

Light Fur Fluffing: A Subtle, Satisfying Stroke

AREA: Side of Dog.
HAND PARTS: Finger pads, fingertips, four fingers.
HAND POSITION: Palm down.
MOTION: Gliding.
SPEED: Slow-mo.
PRESSURES: Featherlight, light.
MOOD: Gentle and relaxed.

TECHNIQUE:

Easy does it here. This technique is full of graceful, flowing caresses. Just like its name, emphasis is on the very tender touch. Use your finger pads, fingertips, and four fingers. With feather-light gliding strokes, keep pressure very light and speed slow-mo. Follow dog contours from shoulder to flank.

No Thanks _____   My Dog Likes _____   My Dog Really Likes _____

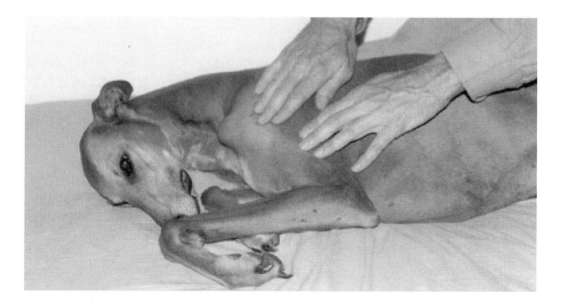

Dog Sandwich

AREA: Both sides of Dog.
HAND PARTS: Open palm, closed palm.
HAND POSITIONS: Palm up, palm down.
MOTION: Gliding.
SPEED: Slow-mo.
PRESSURE: Light.
MOOD: Gentle and relaxed.

TECHNIQUE:

Position one hand under Dog's body at the shoulder. Put your other hand on top of the corresponding shoulder that is facing you, with Dog in the middle.

Glide your hands (open or closed palm) slowly down along both sides of your dog, from shoulders and chest out to rump.

No Thanks _____   My Dog Likes _____   My Dog Really Likes _____

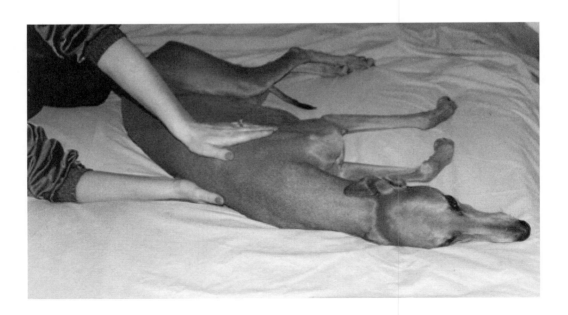

Layla's Luxurious Front-to-Back Caress

AREA: Entire side length of Dog, from front paw to back claw.
HAND PARTS: Four fingers, open palm, closed palm.
HAND POSITIONS: Vertical, horizontal.
MOTION: Gliding.
SPEEDS: Slow-mo, leisurely.
PRESSURES: Light, mild.
MOOD: Gentle and relaxed.

TECHNIQUE:

This technique works best when Dog is lying stretched out on her side. Isn't it amazing how far they can stretch like this?

Start at her front paw (using the hand parts and positions listed), and slowly begin one grand long, flowing glide. Continue up the foreleg, along the shoulder, side, and back down her thigh. Repeat a few times, with you enjoying the feel of Dog, and Dog enjoying the feel of you.

ADVANCED VARIATION:

Start at the tip of her front paw, and end at the tip of her back claw.

Take all the time in the world with this
technique—the slower the better. Sometimes, just when
you think your dog can't grow any longer, she'll stretch
out a few more inches in glorious response and
appreciation of this luxurious caress.

No Thanks _____   My Dog Likes _____   My Dog Really Likes _____

Alternating Circular Side Waving

AREA: Top and broad sides of Dog.
HAND PARTS: Open palm, closed palm, finger pads, fingertips,
    four fingers, thenar eminence, knuckle nooks.
HAND POSITIONS: Vertical, horizontal.
MOTIONS: Circling, rubbing.
SPEEDS: Slow-mo, leisurely, fast 'n' frisky.
PRESSURES: Featherlight, light, mild, deep.
MOODS: Gentle and relaxed, playful, frolicky fun.

TECHNIQUE:

Create large clockwise and counterclockwise circles all over
side of Dog. Become comfortable with one hand, then use both
hands. Simply rub both hands up and down in unison. Than alternate with one hand up closer to the top, the other hand
closer to the belly. Enjoy using the variety of hand parts listed for
this technique. Your dog will guide you through the choices of
pressures and speeds.

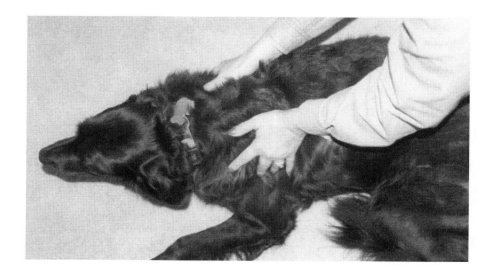

CAUTION

Make sure she permits the fur ruffling that accompanies this technique.

No Thanks _____   My Dog Likes _____   My Dog Really Likes _____

Side Palming

AREA: Sides of Dog.
HAND PARTS: Open palm, closed palm.
HAND POSITIONS: Vertical, horizontal, cupping.
MOTION: Waving.
SPEEDS: Slow-mo, leisurely, fast 'n' frisky.
PRESSURES: Light, featherlight, mild, deep.
MOODS: Gentle and relaxed, playful, frolicky fun.

TECHNIQUE:

Position your hand on Dog's side. Gently press your palm into her/his side and wave back and forth. Wave the length of a few inches. Release pressure, slide to the next spot, and repeat your wave. Your wave may be over a few inches or larger, depending on dog size. As usual, start with light pressure. Use all four pressures. Which does Dog prefer—light, featherlight, mild, or deep?

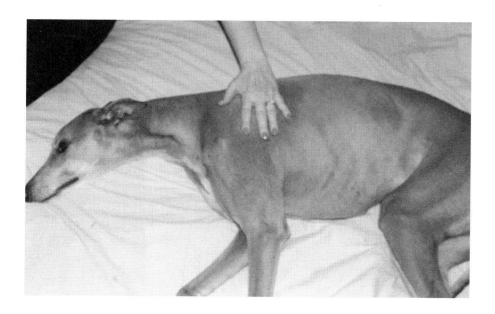

Same with speeds. Start with slow-mo and alternate. Use different speeds. Which does Dog prefer—slow-mo, leisurely, or fast 'n' frisky? Dogs with short hair may have less movement here compared to their thicker-coated counterparts. Furry canines may enjoy having their skin really moved around with this technique. Always pay attention to feedback.

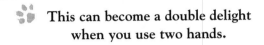 **This can become a double delight
when you use two hands.**

No Thanks _____   My Dog Likes _____   My Dog Really Likes _____

Treasure Chest

The front of your dog provides a veritable treasure chest for massage techniques. So proud of its magnificent chest, many a dog will welcome your attention here.

These are considered more advanced techniques, because you are reaching around and under your dog's head. Be sure you have warmed up your dog with some massage before you approach the chest. And be sure you are extra aware of Unfriendly Feedback signals, and that you heed their message.

Many chest strokes encourage Dog to show off his beautiful furry front. Approach respectfully, carefully, and slowly.

Let's open the treasure chest now!

Chest Techniques

1. Breast Stroking
2. Chest Cupping
3. Buffing the Breastplate
4. Petting the Pecs
5. Underarm Tickle

Breast Stroking

AREA: Chest.
HAND PARTS: Thenar eminence, knuckle nooks, finger pads, fingertips, four fingers, open palm, closed palm, two fingers.
HAND POSITIONS: Horizontal, vertical.
MOTIONS: Waving, strumming, gliding, circling, flicking.
SPEEDS: Slow-mo, leisurely, fast 'n' frisky.
PRESSURES: Featherlight, light, mild, deep.
MOODS: Gentle and relaxed, playful, frolicky fun.

TECHNIQUE:

Simply wave your way around Dog's furry front using all the hand parts listed in a horizontal or vertical position. When your dog raises his head to give you more room, take that as a friendly feedback signal and continue. Do some detailed waving strokes using your fingertips. Horizontally work your way from the bottom of Dog's throat down to and in and around his chest, and under his arms. Then vertically wave across the chest. Add some

gliding, circling, and flicking motions. Advance to strumming. Begin with slow-mo speed and build up to leisurely and perhaps fast 'n' frisky. Do the same with pressures—strum with featherlight pressure, just feeling for fur. Slowly work with light, mild, and then with Dog approval, deep pressure.

VARIATION:

Work the chest area using only featherlight pressure and slow-mo speed. It's tricky to work so slowly and so lightly, and yet it can feel so good.

Be careful never to press deeply on the throat.

CAUTION

No Thanks _____   My Dog Likes _____   My Dog Really Likes _____

Chest Cupping

AREA: Chest.
HAND PARTS: Open palm, closed palm.
HAND POSITION: Cupping.
MOTION: Rubbing.
SPEEDS: No-mo, slow-mo.
PRESSURE: Light, mild.
MOOD: Gentle and relaxed.

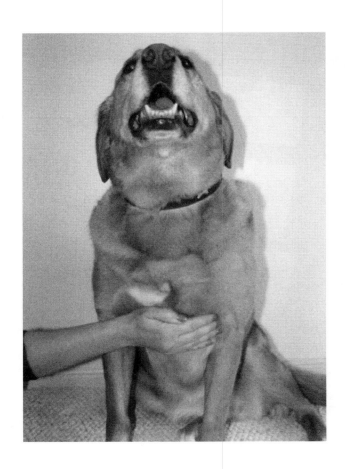

TECHNIQUE:

Simply cup Dog's chest in your palm. Hold it still for a short while. Practice no-mo speed—no action necessary, just companionship.

VARIATION—SLIGHT CHEST SQUEEZING:

Add a slight rubbing squeeze to your hands. If yours is a small dog, your whole palm may cover his chest. If yours is larger, you can squeeze a few times, then reposition your hand and squeeze a few more times, and keep doing this until you've covered the whole chest.

For very large dogs, this can take some time. And since Dog Massage does not rush, take all the time you want.

No Thanks _____   My Dog Likes _____   My Dog Really Likes _____

Buffing the Breastplate

AREA: Center of chest, the bump of his breastplate (sternum).

HAND PARTS: Finger pads, four fingers, fingertips.

HAND POSITIONS: Horizontal, vertical.

MOTIONS: Rubbing, waving.

SPEEDS: Slow-mo, leisurely.

PRESSURES: Light, mild, deep.

MOODS: Gentle and relaxed, playful, frolicky fun.

TECHNIQUE:

Feel the bony protuberance on the front of Dog's chest, in the center of his breastplate. Using the hand parts listed, rub in and around this area—a simple technique. Add some gentle waving if desired. Keep the speed slow-mo to leisurely and alternate the pressures and moods according to your canine's critiques.

No Thanks _____   My Dog Likes _____   My Dog Really Likes _____

Petting the Pecs

AREA: Pectoral muscles on the front of Dog's chest.
HAND PARTS: Closed palm, open palm, finger pads, fingertips.
HAND POSITIONS: Cupping, horizontal, vertical.
MOTIONS: Rubbing, waving, gliding.
SPEEDS: Slow-mo, leisurely.
PRESSURES: Light, mild.
MOODS: Gentle and relaxed, playful.

TECHNIQUE:

When Dog is in position to expose his chest, rub in and around the mighty pectoral muscles, using the hand parts listed. The pecs are the muscles prominently displayed on the chest of body builders. Locate them on your dog.

Cup your palm lightly on his chest in a horizontal or vertical position, and massage this area. Slow waving and gentle gliding can feel good here. Use slow-mo unless Dog requests a faster pace, keep the pressures light to mild, and the moods gentle and relaxed to playful. This technique works equally well on Duke or Duchess.

No Thanks _____   My Dog Likes _____   My Dog Really Likes _____

Underarm Tickle

AREA: Armpit.
HAND PARTS: Finger pads, fingertips, knuckle nooks.
MOTIONS: Rubbing, gliding, circling, waving, flicking.
SPEED: Slow-mo (leisurely and with Dog's approval).
PRESSURES: Light, featherlight.
MOODS: Gentle and relaxed, playful.

🐾 **Once Dog is favorably involved with Dog Massage, then he may be ready for the Underarm Tickle. Best done when Dog is lying on back or side.**

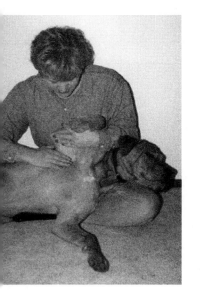

TECHNIQUE:

This is an advanced technique. Make sure your dog is comfortable during Dog Massage, and comfortable with what you're doing, because you and your face are very close to Dog. When done correctly, it is sure to produce a Doggy Grin!

Massage in and around the shoulder and chest areas. Weave your way up to the armpits. Rub back and forth in this area. Glide a bit. Try a few circles, waves, and flicks. Then listen for Doggy Giggles.

VARIATIONS:

Use your fingertips for featherlight flicking, bestowing upon Dog a most unexpected, amusing delight. Extend his front leg up and (with your other hand) gently lift it slightly away from the chest. This gives you more area to massage.

Be extra careful, attentive, and responsive to Dog's critiques, especially Unfriendly Feedback, any time that you're reaching underneath Dog's body.

CAUTION

If your dog enjoys this, his pleasure will be obvious—widespread arms reaching out, telling you that you've done it right again! And that Doggy Grin says you're loved and appreciated.

No Thanks _____   My Dog Likes _____   My Dog Really Likes _____

Thigh Action

The muscles of the thigh are major muscles that provide forward motion. They propel Dog forward. They also enable fantastic Frisbee leaping, sprinting, and jumping.

CAUTION

Some dogs are sensitive about work on their rear end, so follow your Feedback Signals.

Thigh Techniques

1. Thigh Thumbing
2. Post-Exercise Thigh Circles

Thigh Thumbing

AREA: Outside part of the thigh, from the upper hindleg to the spine.
HAND PART: Thumbs.
HAND POSITION: Horseshoe.
MOTION: Rubbing.
SPEEDS: Slow-mo, leisurely.
PRESSURES: Light, mild, deep.
MOOD: Gentle and relaxed.

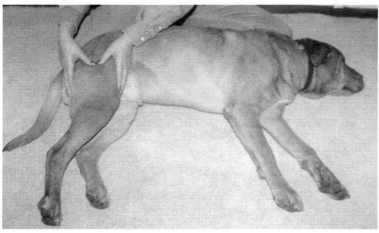

CAUTION

If Dog does not like this technique, move along to the next one.

TECHNIQUE:

With your two hands in a horseshoe position, hold Dog's hindleg. Your pinkie fingers will be closer to the body of the dog, and your thumbs will be closer to the foot. The rubbing motion will be toward the foot. Hold Dog's leg loosely but securely, with the leg resting on your palm and fingers. As if you're twiddling your fingers, slowly start rubbing with your thumbs. Rub thumbs in unison, or alternate. Start slowly and build up speed to leisurely, with Dog's approval. Start with light pressure and alternate with mild and deep. Particularly after a strenuous workout, slow deep work here will help flush out accumulated toxins. Note: When done to flush out toxins, reverse positions, so those strokes are *toward* the main body.

Work the entire leg, starting high up near the body, and continue down to the paws. The closer toward the toes, the lighter you work, because you don't want to be shoving blood into the paws.

You can also do this on the foreleg (Shoulder Thumbing, page 63).

No Thanks _____   My Dog Likes _____   My Dog Really Likes _____

Post-Exercise Thigh Circles

AREA: Thigh.
HAND PARTS: Finger pads, four fingers, open palm, closed
palm.
HAND POSITION: Palm down.
MOTIONS: Circling, rubbing, gliding.
SPEEDS: Slow-mo, leisurely.
PRESSURES: Light, mild, deep with approval.
MOODS: Gentle and relaxed, playful.

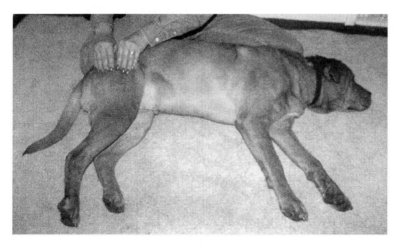

CAUTION

If your dog does not appreciate being touched in this area, move on to another technique.

TECHNIQUE:

This advanced technique helps prevent hip stiffness, particularly after a good workout. It requires extra diligence and patience. It works the powerful thigh muscles that bring the leg forward and back, to remove toxins accumulated from a workout. Work small circles with your finger pads into this area. Use one, two, three, or four finger pads to soothe this muscular area. Keep your circles small, and concentrate on that small area. Add pressure as allowed by your dog. Slowly and carefully rub up and down.

Apply circular pressure in the area where the quadriceps, gluteus medius, and gluteus maximus join together. Be sure to follow your dog's feedback signals. Important: after circling and rubbing, be sure you finish with a few glides up the leg, toward the body. Use four fingers or palms (open or closed) for these glides. Add those upward glides because you want to flush the toxins from that small area.

CAUTION

Some dogs, particularly shorthaired, may not like this technique.

No Thanks _____   My Dog Likes _____   My Dog Really Likes _____

Tummy Touching

Imagine one of a dog lover's favorite images—their wonderful canine, flipped over onto his back and wriggling, legs up in the air, complete with a wide Doggy Grin. Some dogs love their belly rubs, so let's oblige them.

For some dogs, the belly can be Paws Off! territory. If your dog is sensitive or unpredictable here, stop massage.

CAUTION

There may be times when a dog doesn't want Tummy Touching. Call them belly bomber days, when the belly is off-limits. That's fine—there's plenty of other areas to massage, so don't take it as an insult. Simply go elsewhere.

Note: The best belly work begins at the chest level, and from there weave your way down to the tummy area. Avoid starting off low on the abdomen—even a well-massaged mutt appreciates warm-up work here. As with all Dog Massage, start with all slow speed, light pressure, and a gentle and relaxed mood. Progress from there. So, on desirable days, here's what to do for some abdominal action.

Belly Techniques

1. Belly Browsing
2. Stand-Up Stomach Stroking

Belly Browsing

AREA: Belly.
HAND PARTS: Knuckle nooks, open palm, closed palm, four
   fingers, finger pads, fingertips, knuckles.
HAND POSITIONS: Palm down, palm up, cupping, horseshoe.
MOTIONS: Rubbing, circling, waving.
SPEEDS: Slow-mo, leisurely.
PRESSURES: Featherlight, light, mild.
MOODS: Gentle and relaxed, playful, frolicky fun.

If your dog doesn't like abdominal action, skip this technique and skip this chapter.

CAUTION

TECHNIQUE:

Use the techniques of the Treasure Chest (pages 129–137) to
introduce yourself to this area. Warm up the chest area before

proceeding to the belly. Begin at the chest level, with Dog lying on his side or back. Very lightly and very slowly browse around the belly area. Start with some gentle rubbing, using the hand parts listed. Progress with slow waving. Reach around to the sides as well. Start with featherlight pressure and slow-mo speed.

Discover what your dog fancies.

VARIATION—CLOCKWISE CUDDLING: A CANINE CUTIE:

Make belly circles all around Dog's tummy area. Make small ones, the size of a quarter, by barely moving your hand. Then circle larger and wider. Alternate different sizes, and alternate different hand parts. It's soothing, like when a mommy rubs her baby's tummy. Also, keep your dog tickled and your creativity sparked with reverse circles.

No Thanks _____   My Dog Likes _____   My Dog Really Likes _____

Stand-Up Stomach Stroking

AREA: Belly.

HAND PARTS: Finger pads, knuckle nooks, two fingers, finger-tips, four fingers, closed palm, open palm.

HAND POSITION: Palm up.

MOTIONS: Waving, rubbing, circling.

SPEEDS: Slow-mo, leisurely, fast 'n' frisky.

PRESSURES: Light, mild, deep.

MOODS: Gentle and relaxed, playful.

If your dog is not interested, don't pursue it. Some dogs will simply sit down, ending the technique. Go on to another part of the body.

CAUTION

TECHNIQUE:

With Dog standing upright on all fours, feel his belly. Slowly move any of the hand parts listed from side to side in a waving motion. Then add short rubs back and forth. Alternate with circles.

No Thanks _____   My Dog Likes _____   My Dog Really Likes _____

Paws and Claws

Dogs walk on them and you'll hear them clicking across your hardwood floors. They are used for digging holes and for gaining traction during a sprint. They are the Paws and Claws of your dog.

Sometimes we take the magnificence of our own "paws" for granted. Think of the many activities they perform—walking, picking up a phone, turning a key, something as simple as waving good-bye or as important as opening a bag of dog food.

Paws and Claws are always busy, whether it's Duchess having her paws full with a new litter of puppies or Duke outside digging an exquisite new backyard hole.

Anyone who has enjoyed the massage that goes along with a manicure or pedicure remembers its soothing effect on these very active body parts. The same is true for your wonderful dog. However, no pulling on their "fingers." That is not soothing at all and quite undesirable.

The two front legs are called forepaws, and they're the equivalent of our wrist, palm, and fingers. The two back legs are called hindpaws and they correspond to our ankle, foot, and toes.

CAUTION

Paws and Claws can be a sensitive area for a dog, and it takes approval to massage this area. These are considered advanced techniques, so be sure you have warmed up Dog with massage before you touch the toes. Be sure to pay keen attention to Unfriendly Feedback here, and respond immediately. Some dogs will prefer that you skip this chapter entirely. If so, do so.

Paws and Claws Techniques

1. Paw-Claw Caress
2. Paw Sandwich
3. Tiptoeing Through the Toes

Paw-Claw Caress

AREA: Paw pad and claw.

HAND PARTS: Finger pads, finger sides, fingertips, thenar eminence, thumb pads.

HAND POSITIONS: Horizontal, vertical.

MOTIONS: Circling, rubbing.

SPEEDS: No-mo, slow-mo.

PRESSURES: Featherlight, light, mild.

MOOD: Gentle and relaxed.

TECHNIQUE:

Allow Dog's paw pad to rest on your fingers. Let the paw rest there for a few moments of familiarity. Then slowly rotate your fingers in clockwise and counterclockwise motions to feel the entire area of the paw pad. Next rub back and forth from the tip of the claw up to your dog's "wrist," using the hand parts listed. Rub along the "palm" of the paw, and rub the other side, too.

This is a sensitive area, so keep the approach and your touch gentle. Any resistance or out-of-character behavior—stop Dog Massage.

CAUTION

No Thanks _____   My Dog Likes _____   My Dog Really Likes _____

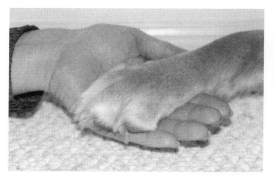 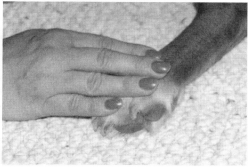

Paw Sandwich

AREA: Paw, top and bottom.
HAND PARTS: Open palm, finger pads, thumb pad.
HAND POSITION: Cupping.
MOTION: Rubbing.
SPEEDS: No-mo, slow-mo.
PRESSURES: Featherlight, light.
MOOD: Gentle and relaxed.

TECHNIQUE:

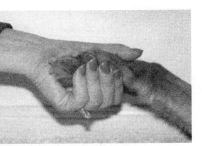

Gently cup Dog's paw within your own open palm. Hold for a moment, and let her get accustomed to this new feel. Add a mild rubbing squeeze, using your finger pads and thumb pad, gauging her response for you to continue. If encouraged, you can even slowly rotate your hand around her paw, twisting back and forth, or slowly up and down. Just a new feel for a familiar area. It's a paw-fect technique on a paw-fect area.

CAUTION

If your dog agrees, fine. If not, don't take it personally—move onto another technique.

No Thanks _____   My Dog Likes _____   My Dog Really Likes _____

Tiptoeing Through the Toes

AREA: Toes.
HAND PARTS: Thumb, finger sides.
HAND POSITION: Palm down.
MOTION: Rubbing.
SPEED: Slow-mo.
PRESSURES: Featherlight, light.
MOOD: Gentle and relaxed.

As with each technique, get Dog's permission before continuing. If there is ever any question, stop massage.

CAUTION

TECHNIQUE:

After warming up with the previous moves, you can approach this detailed technique with confidence. Dog is relaxed and knows she's in good hands with you. So when she gives you her paw freely, feel in and among the individual toes on both her forepaws and hindpaws. Using the sides of your thumb and index finger, slowly rub your way from the base of her toes out to the tips. Then slowly follow each toe up and down. For more variety, move in and around her paw pads. Keep the pressure featherlight to light and the mood gentle and relaxed.

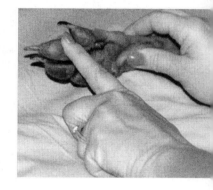

No Thanks _____   My Dog Likes _____   My Dog Really Likes _____

Tail End

Our canine companions are so proud of their furry finales—their tails. Whether fat and fluffy, sleek and flowing, a dog's tail can be his badge of honor. This furry showpiece becomes a display of canine distinction.

The tail corresponds to our sacral bones, and these bones are called the caudal vertebrae. Man has five bones fused together to form the sacrum; the dog has any number of caudal vertebrae, from one or two to twenty-two or more, which extend out to become the tail. While this is literally the tail end of the vertebral column, it's by no means the tail end of Dog Massage. A dog may show his pleasure by holding his tail up for you, and keeping it relaxed and wagging.

CAUTION

If your dog pulls his tail between his legs, or if his tail is tense and tightly held, stop massage. Your dog may prefer for you to skip this chapter. If so, do so.

Tail End Techniques

1. Caudal Cuddling
2. Tail End

Caudal Cuddling

AREA: Tail.
HAND PARTS: Finger pads, thumb.
HAND POSITION: Horseshoe.
MOTION: Rubbing.
SPEEDS: Slow-mo, leisurely.
PRESSURES: Light, mild.
MOOD: Gentle and relaxed.

TECHNIQUE:

Start from the base of the rump and feel along the tail, right out to the tip. With the tail positioned between your four fingers and thumb, gently rub these caudal vertebrae with your finger pads and thumb and follow them out to their natural conclusion.

No Thanks _____   My Dog Likes _____   My Dog Really Likes _____

Tail End

AREA: Tail.
HAND PARTS: Finger pads, open palm, four fingers, thumb.
HAND POSITION: Palm down.
MOTION: Gliding.
SPEEDS: Slow-mo, leisurely.
PRESSURES: Featherlight, light, mild, deep.
MOODS: Gentle and relaxed.

Be sure Dog likes tail attention before you continue. If Dog shows any unfriendly feedback signals, stop massage.

CAUTION

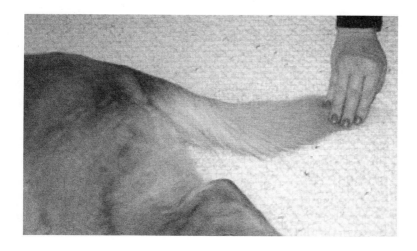

TECHNIQUE:

This is best done as an extension of The Grand *Effleurage* (pages 73–75). Follow the long body stroke right down from the rump and continue out to the tail. Lightly hold the tail in your hand, with finger pads and open palm, or four fingers with thumb support. Gracefully glide right on out to its tip.

For a change of pressure and style, softly add a few squeezes to the tail as you follow along its length. This is a most elegant finishing touch to your massage.

No Thanks _____   My Dog Likes _____   My Dog Really Likes _____